# cooking with coffee

NADINA DARROCH

# cooking with coffee

HART PUBLISHING COMPANY, INC.
NEW YORK CITY

## *acknowledgments*

We wish to acknowledge with gratitude the Brazilian Coffee Institute
for their generous help and courtesy, especially Mr. Helio Guerreiro and Mr. Cesar Gomes,
and the New York Public Library Picture Archives.

# contents

# the main event

# bake with coffee

## *Breads*

## *Cakes and Pastries*

### Cookies and Bars

# perfect endings

# the tops

# coffee confections

# index

# *introduction*

*Coffee has come into general use, as a food in the morning and after dinner as a tonic and exhilarating drink.*
*—The Psychology of Taste,*
Brillat-Savarin

An ocean of coffee has been imbibed since Brillat-Savarin wro his commentary on consumption of the beverage in the court Louis XVI of France. A welcome, steaming tide of the rich, da brew has swept across the world, and has generated an incredil harvest of recipes using the coffee fruit.

Having been exposed to the bubbling-pot syndrome, at an ea ly age, I have always regarded coffee as a necessity on any stap shelf. And, over the past year, I have been enthralled by the ploration of coffee's creative potential in cooking.

The potential of coffee is astonishing! More than just a sip w a zip, coffee is a creative base for a smorgasbord of appetizi dishes. From a subtle flavoring for meats and sauces to the b mocha taste of delectable desserts, the benevolent bean has u versal appeal.

Coffee even boasts its own economies. The recipes in t book eliminate the need to throw away any leftover coffee. Ev spoonful is good to the very last ground—you need never dri another drop of bitter, reheated coffee. Simply jar and refriger leftover coffee until ready to use it as an ingredient in a favo entree, bread, or dessert. The results are deliciously thrifty, w an emphasis on good taste.

# the benevolent bean

harvest time,
Brazilian
workers pour
coffee beans
into sacks for
export.

For sheer intrigue and excitement at the international level, the story of coffee can't be topped. Coffee has gone into battle, coffee has influenced the social thinking of an era, coffee has started riots, and coffee has even been outlawed in free-thinking Sweden. Coffee has been as much talked about as talked over. Aromatic and pleasurable, the fruits of the coffee tree have furnished a luxurious beverage to mankind for over two thousand years.

With its roots deep in African soil, the coffee "cherry" first appeared on man's menu as a food. The ancient Ethiopians crushed raw coffee in enormous stone mortars, then mixed it with animal fat. Rolled into practical, portable balls, the coffee mixture formed a high-protein staple for warriors on the move. This was an ideal food, uniquely suited to its use: an effective, primitive C-ration. Coffee in its raw state has a high protein content; while caffein adds a potent stimulant. The Ethiopian coffee balls definitely had plenty of bounce to the ounce.

The coffee of Abyssinia (modern Ethiopia) was an abundant natural resource. The kaffa trees grew lush in the warm, moist forests. Natives could stroll through great coffee groves, flaying the trees with sticks until the ripe "cherries" fell to the ground. The deep, dark red fruit had a sweet, pleasing taste, and was readily available. The berries were there for picking, just waiting to be swept up by the tides of time. A strong food for strong men, coffee still belonged to the Ethiopians.

Although Africans made wine of fermented juice of the coffee berries, coffee did not appear as a hot beverage until almost 1000 A.D. Brought back from Abyssinia by Arab trade caravans, coffee was introduced into the Moslem world. At first, it had mystical connotations—a powerful, stimulating drink to be sipped sparingly and passed hand to hand by the faithful. As its use spread, coffee still remained a mysterious medicinal brew, to be consumed only on the advise of a physician. The brew was considered far too potent for ordinary consumption.

Gradually, however, coffee entered into the everyday lives of the Arabs, who were quick to see its potential as a commodity. Trade development moved slowly, but steadily. Then, in the early 1500s, Turkish merchants carried fragrant coffee cherries into Constantinople. The bridge into Europe was about to be spanned.

In 1585, Venetian traders brought coffee to Italy. The aromatic, exotic brew gained almost instant popularity among the cosmopolitan Venetians, and stirred up a heated controversy among Catholic priests. Zealots condemned the new craze as a devil's brew sent by the Moslems to corrupt Christians. Condemned or not, a coffee culture was growing. Almost a century after the merchant ships brought back the first coffee cargoes, Venice became the birthplace of Europe's first coffeehouse.

In 1669, the Turkish ambassador to the court of Louis XVI introduced the heavenly brew to France. The Moslem drink delighted the Sun King and his court. Soon, the fashionable fad of coffee-drinking overflowed into the streets of Paris. Vendors hawked their wares from steaming carts, and Parisians flocked to buy. To

*The coffee plant produces delicate blossoms and rich, fragrant berries.*

the average Frenchman, coffee was the great equalizer, enjoyed by king and commoner alike.

By 1689, Paris had its first café. Throughout the 1600s, coffeehouses were to proliferate across the continent. What the salon was to the wealthy, the coffeehouse became for the ordinary man on the street: a meeting place not only for the body, but for the mind.

In Rome, Pope Clement VIII, troubled by the heat of the coffee furor, demanded that coffee be brewed in his chambers. After all, he had a duty to protect his universal flock. The results of the pontiff's experiment would have fulfilled an adman's dream. After one cautious sip, Pope Clement declared that anything so delicious could not conceivably be sinful. With the Pope's blessing, coffee popularity was on its way up.

Across the channel in London, hundreds of coffeehouses had sprung up by the turn of the eighteenth century. The writers and artists who gathered in these new meeting places wielded great influence on the social and political thinking of their time. The world was on the brink of The Age of the Common Man, and coffeehouse meetings gave birth to a new type of communication—the gossipy coffeehouse newspapers. Joseph Addison and Sir Richard Steele captured the thinking of England with their papers, *The Tattler* and *The Spectator*.

Indeed, coffee has been an inspiration to a number of writers. Alexander Pope included a charming canto about the beverage in *The Rape of the Lock*. William Hogarth, the English painter and engraver, chose coffeehouses for a number of satirical social caricatures. Hogarth's *Rake's Progress* and *Four Times a Day* were to become classics. Voltaire joked about coffee. While in Germany,

Johann Sebastian Bach wrote his *Coffee Cantata #211* of the Secular Cantatas, to immortalize coffee in the world of music.

The *Coffee Cantata*, published in Leipzig in 1732, was a light-hearted spoof about the serious medical thinking of the time. Physicians, concerned by the enormous coffee consumption, were warning that coffee-drinking would make women sterile. The idea seemed so ludicrous to Bach, the coffee lover, that it inspired the cantata, a burlesque criticism of the doctors.

Meanwhile, on the Scandinavian penninsula, Swedes were drinking coffee in such fantastic quantities that, in 1754, a law was

*Before the advent of the milling machir*
*hardy agricultural workers milled the beans by har*

passed prohibiting its use. The great Swedish coffee prohibition brought on new excesses—riots, coffee speakeasies, and coffee raids. Predictably, coffee bootlegging ran rampant until popular demand forced the Swedish government to repeal the law. The Swedes' thirst for the brew has remained strong ever since—today, the average Swede consumes thirty pounds of coffee a year!

The trade-conscious Dutch introduced coffee to Java in 1696. As a result, Java and Sumatra, widely planted with coffee by the Dutch East India Company, quickly became a huge coffee-producing area, of key importance to international trade.

In 1720, Mathieu de Clieu, a young French naval officer, through a series of machinations that had all the romantic overtones of a Dumas novel, managed to have the prize coffee tree of Le Jardin des Plantes, in Paris, stolen and smuggled to his plantation on the island of Marinique. After a harrowing sea voyage, enlivened by fierce storms, pirate chases, and a deadly becalming in which de Clieu was forced to share his precious ration of drinking water with the plant, coffee made its successful entrance into the New World.

Charles Lamb, the English writer, immortalized de Clieu's coffee capers in his poem, *The Coffee Slips*, with verses that begin:

> Whene'er I fragrant coffee drink,
> I on the generous Frenchman think,
> Whose noble perseverance bore
> The tree to Martinico's shore.

De Clieu's escapades paid off handsomely. The warm, wet climate of the West Indies made coffee-growing ideal. De Clieu was to live to see his dream of a personal coffee empire grow into the glory of France. The moisture-loving plants thrived in the Western Hemisphere, spreading from Martinique to French Guiana on the South American mainland, and ultimately, on into Brazil.

According to romantic legend, the swashbuckling intrigue of de Clieu's time was repeated when the wife of the governor of French Guiana defied the crown command not to export coffee plants or seeds outside government territories. The king guarded his national coffee advantages jealously. But the story runs that when the governor's wife gave seeds to a charming Brazilian, Sergeant Major Francisco de Melo Palheta, the French coffee monopoly in the Western Hemisphere was broken.

And, in truth, it was. However, history adds an element of more practical—and exciting—truth to a charming legend. De Melo Palheta was under strict government orders from his Brazilian superiors when he brought the famous coffee trees and seeds to Brazil. Brazil had thrown down the gauntlet, challenging the unfair barriers set up by the French to their coffee trade with Brazil. The cleverly manipulated contraband, five plants and more than a thousand seeds, were to furnish a higher level of intrigue than romantic legend can provide. The pattern of coffee as a modern international commodity was being set.

The celebrated French seeds found an excellent environment in northern Brazil. Soon the coveted "green gold" had spread to the eastern and then to the southern parts of the country. In the south, in the state of Sao Paulo, coffee had found its ideal location. Sao Paulo was to become the leading coffee-producing region of Brazil.

The industrial revolution in Europe during the nineteenth century was the key factor in the Brazilian coffee boom. Working in large, new factories radically changed the lives of ordinary people.

*Coffee husks are spread in the sun to dry.*

There was a growing demand for strong, stimulating beverages, and coffee filled the popular need. The United States of America had already opted for coffee during the pre-Revolutionary period. The Boston Tea Party had sped along the colonists' changeover, which came as a direct result of opposition to unfair English taxation. In time, the United States would become the largest coffee market in the world.

The wars of independence in the West Indies also helped lay the groundwork in a situation favorable to the Brazilian boom. But it was not until the mid-1800s, that Brazilian coffee-exporting began to create a dramatic impact on world coffee-production. As large coffee *fazendas* (plantations) developed in place of small landholdings, Brazilian coffee output climbed steadily, until by 1880 it had risen to 50 percent.

As coffee growers began to use more sophisticated agricultural techniques and machinery, production increased. A transition was being made in Brazil's status as a modern world-power in the coffee industry. On a national level, coffee became a leading export, transforming the country's economic policies. The cultivation of coffee became the key factor in generating industrial growth.

The money economy that grew out of coffee production accelerated during the nineteenth century. The abolition of Brazilian slavery and an ever-increasing influx of immigrants to Brazil radically changed the social patterns so long dominated by the self-sufficient landholders. With these social changes came new demands for industrialization to provide the goods needed to clothe and house the freshly-created working class of the country.

Meanwhile, parallel social changes were occuring in the United States. The Civil War closed the great southern port of New Orleans to coffee imports. The ships sailed northward into New York

*Coffee served at the Russian Cafe in the park of the 1867 Paris Industrial Exposition.*

Harbor. With them came cargoes of green coffee, which were to make New York the coffee-trading center of the United States. And, accompanying the green gold were far more remarkable innovations, which were to create an entire new technological revolution.

Up to about 1865, coffee was sold green on the consumer market. The roasting was completely dependent on the consumer's ability to prepare the green beans, and the resultant tastes were predictably haphazard. A Philadelphia shipping magnate, John Arbuckle, had the foresight to envision his green gold cargoes roasted and put on the shelves as a prepackaged product. In true Yankee tradition, Arbuckle fulfilled his dream, creating an astonishing marketing revolution. For the first time, it was possible to standardize the taste and aroma of coffee in enormous quantities. With the elimination of the variables of uneven taste and the slow roasting and milling at home, the public began to consume coffee with increasing enthusiasm. A new era had begun.

By the twentieth century, coffee had become a "must" in the daily lives of people all over the world. Today, the coffee bean is a major economic force. The coffee break is a way of life to the American work force, as essential as afternoon tea to the British. Unions have fought long and hard for the right to take a coffee break. Coffee price fluctuations have made the market tremble. As a commodity, coffee has developed a powerful punch.

Today, beautiful, rolling orchards of coffee trees in blossom furnish breathtaking vistas in coffee-growng areas of the world. As delicately fragrant as jasmine, the fragile, coral-white blossoms create a spectacular panorama, a showy prelude to the fruits to come. Nothing has been left to chance in the coffee industry. From countryside to market shelf, every step has been planned.

Coffee culture has become vastly complex, requiring highly specialized and demanding farm techniques. The chronological caravan has carried the benevolent bean a long way from the lush forests of ancient Abyssinia to its twentieth-century hallowed status. Now, armies of scientists have replaced the fierce Ethiopian warriors, marching in constant search of new potentials for coffee use.

Meanwhile, in the fields, the coffee producer cannot afford to gamble with nature. After the first coffee research center was founded in the Brazilian state of Sao Paulo, students and coffee specialists came there from all over the world. Methods of farming became increasingly more scientific, making sporadic crops, which had plagued nineteenth-century growers, obsolete. Radical changes in farming insure a predictable crop, which is essential to successful coffee production and quality.

Since Brazil is the world's leading producer of coffee, the Brazilians have led the way in advancing dramatic new techniques in coffee culture, from the nursery, where the tender seedlings are produced and nurtured, through the harvesting, washing, and drying of the cherries, and beyond, to the roasting and commercial export of the beans. Each stage of development is of equal importance; there is an elaborate series of way stations before coffee reaches our tables.

From the first clusters of green cherries on the trees to harvest time when the boughs are laden with deep-red fruit, the crop is guarded carefully. Inside that sweet red pulp are the pits, or beans, which are the lifeblood of the industry. A coffee tree takes an average of four to five years to mature to a useful harvesting capacity. On maturation, a single tree produces only five pounds of cherries each year.

*Dinner-table coffee-drinking scene, as depicted in 1900, by F.A. Frillbert.*

During the harvest, an experienced picker can gather 200 to 250 pounds of cherries. Each cherry must be painstakingly hand-picked, with great care being taken not to damage the fruit. After the baskets are filled, the picker must take them to be emptied into waiting trucks or animal-drawn wagons. The harvested cherries must then be winnowed, or sifted, as a preliminary cleaning process, before being swept into tanks that are designed to thoroughly wash the fruit with streams of running water. This process washes the cherries free of all foreign particles—sticks, leaves, or gravel—prior to the drying process.

Spread in thin layers on special drying grounds, the cleaned cherries dry in the air and sun for about two to three weeks. During the day, workers turn the berries gently with rakes to insure even drying. At night, the fruit must be heaped into piles and covered to protect it from moisture. In the morning, the spreading process is repeated, until the cherries are thoroughly dried. When dry, the fruit is transferred to milling machines, which remove the dried-up husk, parchment, and the inner silver skin that surrounds the twin beans.

After the milling process, the five pounds of coffee cherries yield one pound of green coffee. Roasting will again reduce the weight. The commercial yield of one tree for an entire year is slightly less than one pound of roasted coffee. A family of two, consuming one pound of coffee per week, will use more than the total annual production of 52 trees in a year. Multiplied by the world's coffee consumption, the demands on the industry are mind-boggling.

Major coffee-producing countries like Brazil, the world's leader, and other important nations, such as Colombia and Mexico, annually spend billions on further scientific development and refinements of what has to be the world's most popular agronomy. While the scientists search out new benefits, food economists are doing major experimenting in the hospitality industry. Coffee can fit into menus from main dishes through breads to cakes and mouthwatering desserts. A symbol of cordial hospitality and warm friendship, coffee—or *café*, *kaffa*, *kawa*, *or kahvi*—is the darling of the world.

Whole rituals of entertaining have evolved around the serving of coffee. The Arabs have a very formalized coffee ceremony, which often begins in a room totally designed for the occasion. The "coffee room" is simplicity in itself. Its main feature is a round fireplace sunk into the floor for preparing the coffee. One person is appointed the coffee maker, and is seated next to the host beside the fireplace. The rest of the guests sit in order of importance, away from the fire and their host. The furnishings are modest by our standards—Oriental carpets and scattered cushions for the guests' comfort.

The coffee maker begins with the green beans, which he heats on a special perforated ladle over the embers. As the beans crackle and roast to a familiar deep brown, the coffee maker places them on a platter. When enough beans are roasted to begin the next step, they are put into a mortar and roughly crushed. The pot, or *ibrik*, is filled with warm water, and the coffee grounds are put on to boil. Even the boiling is a ritual; the liquid must be brought to a boil three times.

While the coffee is being prepared, the guests engage in comfortable small talk, sipping water and eating dates dipped in butter. When the coffee is finally brewed to the maker's satisfaction, the pouring ritual begins. Each demitasse cup, is heated, in turn, by pouring a bit of hot coffee from cup to cup. That portion of the

*Ripe coffee berries must be painstakingly plucked from the tree.*

coffee is poured onto the fire as a libation to the spirit of coffee drinking. At long last, the coffee maker is ready to serve the guests, beginning with the host.

While few modes of entertaining with coffee are as elaborate as the Arabian custom, the convivial German custom of the kaffee klatsch is still very much with us. What could be more hospitable than a well-set afternoon table, laden with steaming pots of fragrant coffee and a delectable selection of cakes, breads, and pastries? More than just another get-together for companionable gossip, the kaffee klatsch can be as sumptuous as a British high tea—or as simple as a coffee and danish. It is well-designed to fit a hostess's mood and budget.

Coffee fits so neatly into our schedules that we are very likely to overlook some of the little niceties that have grown up around it. The day that begins with a continental breakfast somehow feels a bit brighter. A croissant, a dab of butter, a splash of jam, and a piping hot cup of aromatic coffee accompanied by a pitcher of fresh milk—the French *café complet*—is as popular on this side of the ocean as on the other. While we may not all become *boulevardiers* and idle away our coffee breaks at a sidewalk café, American coffee shops thrive on such morning and afternoon breaks—the nice little pick-me-up that refreshes.

In Normandy, where apples abound, the traditional drink is Calvados, a brandylike hard cider. The French farmers of that region prefer a sturdier cup of coffee, and mix theirs accordingly. Half coffee and half Calvados packs a potent punch of brew, indeed! For a down-to-earth accompaniment, the ubiquitous long loaf of French bread should be broken off in hearty chunks, and dunked in the coffee for flavoring.

Across the North Sea, Scandinavian families would feel less

than hospitable if they did not offer their guests a veritable smorgasbord of delicious baked goods with their coffee. Even the poorest household seems to manage at least a plate of homebaked cookies to nibble with the coffee. With traditional Scandinavian appreciation of good food, a whole kitchen culture of delightful coffeecakes and breads have developed, supplying enough recipes to fill a five-foot shelf of cookbooks.

When in Rome do as the Romans do, and head for a picturesque sidewalk café to sip espresso or enjoy a cappuccino. Served in demitasse cups, with a twist of lemon, the dark, delightful espresso is far stronger than our own American brews. Cappuccino is served in tall, slender mugs. "Un cappuccio" combines two-thirds espresso and one-third hot milk, topped with a sprinkling of cinnamon, nutmeg, or perhaps some grated chocolate.

Among certain African tribes, your hostess might very well *feed* you your coffee. Raw beans, macerated in spices and water, make a tasty, tempting treat, to be chewed like candy. And, in a society remote from the electric blender, the mortar and pestle might provide another local favorite, a purée of bananas and raw coffee cherries. Not only a delicious sweet, but chockful of protein as well; in its natural state, the coffee cherry has 14 percent protein.

Throughout the western world, after-dinner coffee is a tradition. Whether served in the customary fashion, simply as a cup of coffee to be taken with milk or sugar; or, as a plain demitasse of dark-roasted French or Italian coffee; or, as a blend of coffee and liquor, coffee is the classic mark of the end of a meal. Coffee can be taken at the dinner table with dessert, or formalized in true drawing-room fashion. While today, few of us enjoy the luxury of a drawing room, the custom of after-dinner coffee can be equally

*Alfresco American coffee break, circa 1890.*

satisfying around the living room coffee table, a warm friendly way to cap the pleasures of the evening meal.

As we take our morning "cuppa" coffee to start the day out right, so we end the evening with the beverage that symbolizes a feeling of well-being and tranquility. Throughout the day, the brown stream flows, dividing up the hours into peaceful moments, punctuating the breaks in the business of our lives. Fads in taste may come and go; but coffee-drinking is here to stay. So, settle back, relax—and, "let's have another cup of coffee—let's have another piece of pie."*

*From song of the same title by Irving Berlin.

# take a break
## Coffee—Plain & Fancy

*For lo! the board with cups and spoons is crown'd,*
*The berries crackle, and the mill turns round;*
*On shining altars of Japan they raise*
*The silver lamp; the fiery spirits blaze;*
*From silver spouts the grateful liquors glide,*
*While China's earth receives the smoaking tyde . . .*
  *—The Rape of the Lock,* Canto III
  Alexander Pope

# the coffee makers

Before you can brew a perfect cup of coffee, you must know your coffee maker. Whether it is a percolator or a drip pot, a cone brewer, or an electric-filter-drip pour-over device, the manufacturer's directions should be followed exactly. The manufacturer has spent years of time and effort in improving his product for your benefit, and he wants to pass on the knowledge to you.

While the Arabian method of coffee still boils the brew, our own tastes dictate the axiom "never boil coffee." That is why today so many people are moving away from percolator coffee. A percolator, by its very design, must boil the coffee in order to make it perk. Therefore, drip methods of coffee brewing are becoming more important to the American scene.

The electric-filter-drip pot is becoming increasingly popular. Long familiar to office workers, the pour-over brewers are finding their way into homes all over the country. The electric-drip maker uses a disposable paper filter, and provides one of the best methods of bringing out the excellent flavor and aroma of fine coffee blends. The procedure is effortless and almost instantaneous.

The original drip pot consists of two sections, with a perforated basket between for the coffee grounds. With or without filter paper, nothing could be simpler than pouring the boiling water into the upper cylinder, and letting it filter through the coffee

*...modern electric cappuccino machine ...uces two demi-tasse cups every ...conds.*

grounds into the lower serving section. It can be used with dark French or Italian roasts to produce a creditable—if not quite authentic—espresso.

The glass-cone brewers are, perhaps, the simplest of the coffee makers. The device produces a superior cup of coffee if precise measurements are made. A paper or cloth filter screens out any residue of the grounds, leaving only the clear, dark delight of the coffee. As with the double-drip pot, the glass-cone required merely the pouring of boiling water over the grounds. The glass-cone brewer is an excellent and fairly inexpensive brewer for beginning to explore the many delights of sophisticated areas of coffee drinking. Superb Brazilian *cafézinho* can be produced with this brewer, and is well worth trying.

Espresso machines come under the luxury category: they are quite expensive. The principle behind the espresso machine is exactly what the name tells us. These are quick brewers—expresses. The coffee is the product of the force of hot water and steam, under pressure, through the coffee grounds. Espresso coffee is a much stronger brew than ordinarily used, measuring three tablespoons of dark roasted French or Italian coffee per cup. Therefore, it is better for the average coffee drinker to achieve the same effect with an electric pour-over drip pot, or a plain drip maker.

The most important thing for any coffee drinker to keep in mind is that a perfect cup of coffee is a highly individual taste. Follow the basic rules laid down in "How to Make Perfect Coffee," and allow your own taste to dictate the measurements. Once you have determined exactly the strength of coffee you prefer, stick with it. That way, you will consistently make a perfect cup of coffee—clear, full-bodied, and aromatic.

# how to make perfect coffee

Perfect coffee is a rich, clear medium-to-dark brown, and has a deliciously fragrant aroma. It is full-bodied in flavor, without a bitter taste. Perfect coffee is easier to make than you may think, if you follow a few basic rules.

Keep the coffee pot immaculately clean. An absolutely stainless pot is the beginning of a good cup of coffee.

Use only fresh, quality coffee, selecting the grind suited to your coffee maker.

To insure freshness, buy your favorite blend of coffee in small quantities. Store in an airtight container in the refrigerator.

Draw fresh, cold water for each new pot. Do not let the water stand for hours before you begin.

Grounds and water must be measured precisely. Use the coffee measurements in the following chart as a guide. Never skimp.

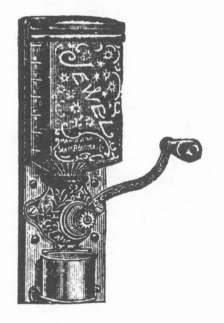

## Coffee Measurements Guide

(applicable to all grinds of regular brown roast coffee)

| Servings | Coffee | Water |
|---|---|---|
| 2 | 4 level tablespoons* | 1½ measuring cups |
| 4 | 8 level tablespoons | 3 measuring cups |
| 6 | 12 level tablespoons | 4½ measuring cups |
| 8 | 16 level tablespoons | 6 measuring cups |
| 10 | 20 level tablespoons | 7½ measuring cups |
| 20 | ½ pound | 1 gallon |
| 40 | 1 pound | 2 gallons |

When using a percolator, time perking carefully. Coffee should be done perfectly 8 minutes after pot begins to perk. NEVER LET COFFEE BOIL.

Remove percolator from heat, and allow to settle before pouring.

In using an electric coffee maker, follow manufacturer's directions.

*2 level tablespoons equal 1 standard coffee measure.

# coffee beverages

## brazilian coffee

### cafézinho

Perfect cafézinho should be made with a dark-roasted coffee. However, if you prefer the lighter roasts, you can still brew a good demitasse of cafézinho.

Measure 4 ounces of cold water for each cup. Place water into saucepan and bring to a full boil.

Place one full measure (2 level tablespoons) of coffee per cup into a cafézinho bag.*

Hold the cafézinho bag over a coffeepot and pour the boiled water into bag.

Hold the bag over pot until all the water has seeped through the coffee.

Serve at once in demitasse cups. Sugar to taste.

*Because cafézinho bags are not readily available in most locales, you can make one of your own by lining the coffee grounds container of your drip pot with a soft flannel bag.

## mexican coffee

    2  cups thick hot chocolate, sweetened
       to taste
 1½  cups strong hot coffee
    ½  teaspoon cinnamon

       Topping:
    ½  cup heavy cream
    ¼  teaspoon nutmeg
    ¼  teaspoon cinnamon
    1  tablespoon superfine sugar

Prepare topping first. Combine cinnamon, nutmeg, and sugar with cream. Whip until cream is stiff and peaky.

Combine hot chocolate, coffee, and cinnamon, and pour into heated cups.

Top each cup with a generous serving of spiced whipped cream.

Makes 4 cups.

## irish coffee

- 4 cups strong hot coffee
- 6 jiggers Irish whiskey
- 6 teaspoons sugar
- 4 tablespoons whipped cream

Combine coffee and sugar, stirring to dissolve sugar.

Add Irish whiskey, stir again, and serve in heated mugs.

Top each mug with a tablespoon of whipped cream.

Makes four mugs.

## spicy viennese coffee

- 4 cups strong hot coffee
- 2 cinnamon sticks
- 4 whole cloves
- ½ teaspoon allspice

  Topping:
- ½ cup heavy cream
- 1 tablespoon sugar
- ½ teaspoon cinnamon

Prepare topping first. Whip together cream and sugar and chill until ready to serve.

In small saucepan, heat, BUT DO NOT BOIL, coffee combined with cinnamon sticks, cloves, and allspice. Gently heat for 10 minutes, to steep. Strain and pour into glass mugs.

Top with whipped cream and sprinkle with cinnamon.

Makes 4 mugs.

## iced mocha supreme

2 squares bittersweet chocolate
4 tablespoons superfine sugar
1 cup hot, strong coffee
¼ cup coffee liqueur
4 cups milk
  whipped cream

Melt chocolate in top of double boiler over boiling water. Add sugar, stirring until sugar is thoroughly dissolved.

Gradually pour in coffee, stirring constantly.

Scald milk in separate pan. Add milk to mocha mixture. Cook until smooth, about 10 minutes.

Remove pan from heat. Stir in coffee liqueur, and chill for at least 3 hours.

Serve beverage in chilled glasses, topped with whipped cream.

Makes 6 glasses.

## bahia iced coffee

1½ jiggers coffee liqueur
1 teaspoon superfine sugar
½ cup strong black coffee
  ice cubes

Combine all ingredients, except ice cubes, in blender and mix at high speed. Serve over ice cubes.

Makes 1 glass.

## cold café au lait

1 *pint strong coffee*
2 *cups sweet, fresh milk*
1 *tablespoon superfine sugar*

Prepare coffee ahead of time and cool. Pour cooled coffee into sectioned ice-cube tray, and freeze hard.

When cubes are frozen, remove 8 or 10 cubes. Put cubes into container of blender. Add milk and sugar.

Blend at high speed until ice is completely dissolved. Mixture will be light and creamy.

Pour into tall chilled glasses. If desired, top with whipped cream. Serve immediately.

Makes 4 glasses.

## mexicali fizz

½ *cup strong cold coffee*
½ *cup instant cocoa mixed with cold milk*
½ *teaspoon cinnamon*
1 *cup pale dry ginger ale*

Combine coffee, instant chocolate drink, and cinnamon. Mix well.

Add ginger ale. Serve beverage in chilled glasses.

If desired, top with whipped cream dusted with nutmeg.

Makes 4 glasses.

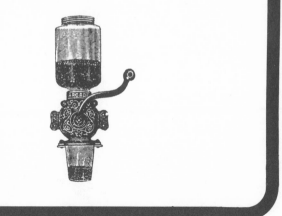

## coffee punch alexander

    2  quarts prepared eggnog
    1  quart (4 cups) very strong, cold coffee
    2  quarts coffee ice cream, softened
    2  cups brandy

Combine all ingredients in a large punch bowl,
stirring mixture until smooth and creamy.
If desired, add small block of coffee ice.

Makes 22 punch cups.

*Coffee Ice:*
In a freezer tray with dividers removed, pour
sweetened black coffee, to fill. Freeze solid, and
use in punch to chill.

## coffee frosted

    1  pint strong cold coffee
    1  pint vanilla ice cream

Chill glasses before serving time.

When ready to serve, beat ingredients together (a
blender is ideal for this) at high speed, until
mixture is light and foamy.

Makes 4 servings.

## mocha frosted

    1  pint strong, cold coffee
    1  pint chocolate ice cream
    4  teaspoons chocolate syrup

Chill glasses ahead of time.

When ready to serve, beat all ingredients together
at high speed until light and foamy.

Makes 4 servings.

## carioca iced coffee

    5 jiggers dark rum
    5 teaspoons sugar
    3 cups very strong cold coffee

Make coffee ahead of time, sweeten with sugar, and chill.

When ready to serve, pour coffee over cracked ice in old-fashioned glasses.

Makes about 4 glasses.

## early bird egg nog

**(a delicious breakfast in a glass)**

    3 cups ice cold coffee *
    1 cup cold milk
    ¼ cup superfine sugar
    4 eggs, well-beaten
    2 teaspoons vanilla extract

Beat eggs well and add vanilla extract.

Combine the milk, coffee, and sugar. Gradually add the milk-and-coffee mixture to the eggs, continuing to beat until frothy.

Serve in tall, chilled glasses.

Makes 4 glasses.

*Note: This recipe is better if the coffee has been well chilled in the refrigerator before preparing.

*The American Café was a lively gathering place at the Paris Exhibition of 1867*

## coffee-banana float

1 ripe banana
1 cup strong, cold coffee
½ cup heavy cream
3 teaspoons superfine sugar
1 cup milk
3 scoops coffee ice cream

Mash banana thoroughly with a fork. Add the coffee, cream, sugar, milk, and vanilla. Beat well with rotary beater or in electric blender at high speed.

Pour into 3 tall, chilled glasses and add a scoop of coffee ice cream to each glass.

Makes 3 tall glasses.

## coffee-apricot shake

1 16-oz. can apricot halves
½ cup strong, ice cold coffee
1 cup table cream
½ pint vanilla ice cream

Combine drained apricot halves, coffee and cream in electric blender. Blend at high speed until well mixed.

Gradually add ice cream, blending after each addition. Mixture will be light and frothy.

Serve in tall, chilled glasses.

For variation, use drained peach slices and peach ice cream.

Makes 4 servings.

# *the main event*
## Coffee in entrees, sauces, and glazes

*Cooking is like love. It should be entered into
with abandon or not at all.*
     —Harriet Van Horne

## tipsy chicken

### (stove-top skillet casserole

     2  chickens, cut into serving pieces
    ½  cup corn oil
     2  large ripe tomatoes, peeled and chopped
     2  large onions, sliced
    ½  lb. lean boiled ham, diced
     1  cup sherry
     1  cup very strong cold coffee
    ¼  cup granulated sugar
    ¼  teaspoon cinnamon
    ¼  teaspoon ground cloves
    ⅛  teaspoon nutmeg
    ⅓  cup seedless raisins

In large skillet, fry chicken in hot oil, until skin turns golden brown.

Add tomatoes and onion, and continue to fry about 10 minutes longer, stirring constantly.

Add remaining ingredients, and mix until well blended with pan juices.

Cover pan and simmer over reduced heat for 20 minutes, or until chicken is done.

Serve chicken on bed of rice.

Serves 6 generously.

## beef brazilia

### (stove-top skillet casserole)

     3  lbs. chuck steak cut into cubes
    ¼  cup (½ stick) butter
     1  tablespoon minced garlic (softened in water)
     3  medium onions, sliced thin
    ¼  cup flour
     1  cup red wine
     2  teaspoons salt
    ½  teaspoon pepper
    ¼  teaspoon oregano
     1  cup strong coffee

Melt butter in deep, heavy skillet. Sauté steak, browning on all sides.

Drain minced garlic. Add garlic and sliced onions to skillet. Cook until onions are soft and transparent.

Remove meat and onions from skillet. Blend flour with remaining butter in skillet.

Gradually add wine, coffee, and seasonings, stirring constantly, until creamy, smooth, and thickened.

Return meat and onions to sauce. Cover and bring to a boil. Reduce heat and simmer for 1½ hours, or until meat is fork-tender.

Serves 6.

## spicy beef brisket

4 lbs. boneless beef brisket
10 or more whole cloves
2 tablespoons peppercorns, coarsely crushed
2 tablespoons vegetable oil
1 cup very strong coffee
1 cup sour cream

Score brisket with a sharp knife, making diamond patterns on both sides of meat. Insert a clove into each diamond.

Put peppercorns in a cloth or paper bag, and crush with a hammer. Press coarsely-crushed peppercorns onto both sides of meat.

In dutch oven, or heavy kettle, brown meat in oil, beginning with fat side. Add coffee, cover, and simmer for 2½ hours, or until meat is tender.

Remove beef from kettle. Keep meat warm while preparing gravy.

Serves 8 generously.

*Spicy Gravy:*

Bring pan juices to a boil, cooking until reduced to 1 cup. Reduce heat. Stir in sour cream, blending well.

Serve over thinly-sliced brisket.

## pork stew mediterranean

2 lbs. lean pork, cubed
½ teaspoon garlic salt
   dash of pepper
3 tablespoons olive oil
1 cup uncooked rice
2 onions, diced fine
4 large ripe tomatoes, peeled and chopped
1 teaspoon granulated sugar
1½ teaspoons salt
2 tablespoons chopped parsley flakes
1 teaspoon ground rosemary
1½ cups water
½ cup strong coffee

Season pork with garlic salt and pepper.

In heavy skillet, brown pork in hot oil.

Reduce heat, and continue cooking for 20 minutes. Remove pork to platter.

Put rice, onions, tomatoes, sugar, salt, and herbs in skillet. Stir constantly over low heat for 3 minutes, to blend thoroughly.

Add browned pork cubes, water, and coffee to casserole with rice and vegetable mixture. Stir to mix thoroughly.

Bake at 325° for 1 hour, or until pork is fork-tender. Rice will absorb the liquid.

Serve with a tossed green salad.

Serves 4 generously.

## glazed breast of lamb

4 lbs. breast of lamb
3 tablespoons minced garlic
1 bottle (8 oz.) oil-and-vinegar salad dressing
6 whole cloves
⅔ cup strong coffee
½ stick butter
2 tablespoons soy sauce
¼ cup honey or brown sugar
2 teaspoons cinnamon

Trim excess fat from meat and cut into 2-rib pieces. Sprinkle both sides with garlic. Marinate meat for 2 hours in oil-and-vinegar salad dressing.

Meanwhile, prepare the barbecue sauce. In small, heavy saucepan, over low heat, combine all ingredients, and simmer for about 10 minutes.

Remove pan from heat, and set aside to steep until cool. Remove cloves from sauce.

Place breast of lamb in a shallow baking dish. Bake at 350°, turning several times, for about 1 hour. Baste and brush frequently with barbecue sauce during the final 30 minutes of baking. Meat is done when tender and crispy brown.

Serves 4.

## coffee-glazed canadian bacon

1 *3-lb. piece of Canadian bacon*
1 *large navel orange, sliced*
  *whole cloves*
½ *cup cider, or apple brandy*
½ *cup very strong coffee*
½ *cup molasses*
¾ *cup brown sugar, firmly packed*
2 *teaspoons dry mustard*

Remove wrapper from Canadian bacon. Place, uncovered, in shallow baking pan, and bake at 325° for 45 minutes.

Remove bacon from oven, and garnish with crescent slices of orange held on by cloves.

Mix the cider with coffee, molasses, brown sugar, and mustard. Bring to boil over low heat, and continue cooking for 3 minutes.

Pour sauce over bacon, reserving some for additional basting. Return bacon to oven and continue baking an additional 50-60 minutes, basting frequently.

Serves 8.

## meatballs carioca

  2 lbs. chuck, chopped
  3 medium onions, chopped fine
¼ stick butter
  1 cup herb-seasoned stuffing mix
  2 eggs
¼ cup cold coffee
  1 teaspoon monosodium glutamate (MSG)
  1 tablespoon garlic salt
    dash of pepper
¼ cup (½ stick) butter
  4 tablespoons flour, or enough to thicken
  1 cup beef broth (one can)

Sauté onions in ¼ stick butter until soft and translucent, BUT NOT BROWNED. Remove from heat.

In large bowl, mix onions with stuffing mix, coffee, MSG, eggs, and ground beef. Mix well to blend. Add pepper and garlic salt.

Form meat into balls and brown in ½ stick butter over low heat.

Remove meatballs from skillet with slotted spoon. Set meatballs aside on platter.

Pour off all but 3 tablespoons pan grease. Gradually add flour to form a smooth paste. Slowly stir into beef broth to form gravy.

Return meatballs to pan and simmer for 10 minutes, or to preferred degree of doneness.

Serve on a bed of hot buttered noodles.

Serves 6 generously.

## brazilian roast pork sauce
### (for basting and gravy)

⅔ cup strong coffee
⅔ stick butter
  2 tablespoons Worcestershire sauce
1¼ teaspoons dry mustard
  1 tablespoon lemon juice
  1 teaspoon ground cloves
  1 teaspoon sugar
    dash of tabasco sauce to taste
    a little flour to thicken

Combine all ingredients, except flour, in heavy saucepan. Heat over low heat until butter melts, stirring frequently.

Brush sauce over roast of pork until it cakes and becomes crispy brown.

Thicken remaining sauce with flour, and serve in sauceboat.

## pot au feu caribe

  2 *lbs. lean beef chuck, cubed*
  2 *lbs. lean pork, cubed*
  1 *lb. ripe tomatoes, peeled and diced*
  2 *large onions, sliced thin*
  2 *bay leaves*
  4 *cloves garlic*
3-4 *lbs. roasting chicken, cut up*
 12 *cups beef or chicken broth*
 ¾ *cup strong black coffee*
  1 *lb. small red potatoes, peeled and sliced*
  1 *lb. string beans, sliced*

In large kettle, place beef, pork, onions, tomatoes, bay leaves, garlic cloves, and stock. Bring to a boil.

Reduce heat and simmer slowly for 1¼ hours. Skim off fat with a slotted spoon.

Add the chicken pieces, coffee, potatoes, and beans. Continue to cook slowly, simmering until meats and vegetables are tender, about 40 minutes. Add salt and pepper to taste.

Serve in large soup plates with plenty of broth.

Delicious with a tossed green salad and crusty French bread.

Serves 8 generously.

# finnish roast lamb

## (lampaanpaisti)

4-5 *lbs. leg of lamb*
3 *cloves garlic, slivered*
2 *tablespoons prepared mustard*
10 *small white onions*
8-12 *fresh baby carrots, (3-4 inches), scrubbed*
10 *small potatoes, peeled*
1 *tablespoon salt*
1 *cup strong coffee*
1 *tablespoon sugar*
1 *tablespoon cream*
2 *beef bouillon cubes, if necessary*

*Sauce:*
1½ *cups pan juice*
1 *tablespoon all-purpose flour*
1 *teaspoon salt*
⅛ *teaspoon pepper*
¼ *cup water*
10 *medium mushrooms, sliced*
1 *teaspoon prepared mustard*

Cut several slits in lamb, and insert garlic slices. Rub lamb with 2 tablespoons mustard. Place lamb in a large roasting pan, and arrange vegetables around roast.

Bake at 425° until surface becomes well-browned, about 15 minutes.

Remove pan from oven, and lower heat to 325°.

Rub lamb with salt. Pour heated coffee, mixed with sugar and cream, over lamb, and return to oven.

Bake about 2 hours. Lamb should be slightly pink in the middle.

Baste with pan juices every 20 minutes. If liquid cooks away, add water mixed with bouillon cubes when necessary.

Turn vegetables occasionally, to prevent scorching.

Remove pan from oven and set aside, covering pan until sauce is prepared.

Serves 8 generously.

*Sauce:*

Strain pan juices through sieve and pour into heavy saucepan. If necessary, add enough water to make 1½ cups. Bring juices to boil.

Meanwhile, mix flour and water to form a smooth paste. Stir flour mixture into saucepan, whisking vigorously to prevent scorching.

Add thinly-sliced mushrooms.

Simmer, stirring constantly, until sauce thickens.

Season with mustard, salt, and pepper to taste. Serve in gravy boat.

Serves 8 generously.

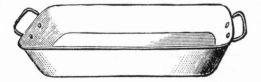

## *charcoal broiled lamb steaks*

    4  *lamb steaks, 1 inch thick*
    3  *cloves of garlic, crushed*
    ½  *cup dry red wine*
    ¼  *cup very strong coffee*
    ¼  *cup vegetable oil*
    ¼  *teaspoon rosemary*
    ¼  *teaspoon thyme*
    ¼  *teaspoon savory*
    1  *teaspoon salt*
    ⅛  *teaspoon black pepper*

Rub steaks on both sides with crushed garlic.

In medium-sized bowl, mix together all remaining ingredients.

Place lamb steaks in a shallow baking pan and pour marinade over them. Marinate for 3 hours, turning frequently.

When steaks are ready to broil, place them on an outdoor grill. Reserve the marinade, basting frequently while meat is broiling.

Broil about 10 minutes on each side. Steaks should be pink and tender on the inside.
Serves 4.

## stuffed barbecued frankfurters

    1  *8 oz. can tomato sauce*
    1  *tablespoon sugar*
    1  *teaspoon basil*
  ½  *teaspoon tarragon*
  ¼  *cup black coffee*
 2-3  *drops tabasco sauce, to taste*
    1  *tablespoon minced garlic*
    1  *lb. frankfurters (8 or 9 franks)*
    4  *large onions, chopped fine*
    3  *tablespoons butter*
 8-9  *slices of bacon*

In small saucepan, combine tomato sauce, sugar, basil, tarragon, coffee, tabasco, and minced garlic. Heat over low heat, stirring well to blend flavors, about 15 minutes. Remove pan from heat.

In a separate skillet, sauté onions in butter.

Meanwhile, split frankfurters lengthwise. With a pastry brush, brush inside each frankfurter with barbecue sauce. Place sautéed onions in each frankfurter and wrap with a bacon slice. Fasten bacon firmly with wooden picks or metal poultry skewers.

Broil franks in oven, turning and brushing frequently with barbecue sauce until bacon is crisp.

Serve in heated frankfurter rolls, or on a bed of baked beans.

*Note: This recipe is also ideal for cookouts. Grill frankfurters 6 inches above coals until bacon is crisp, and serve.*

## liver deluxe
### (with coffee-wine sauce)

    1  *lb. thin-sliced liver (beef or calves)*
    1  *medium onion, thin-sliced*
    3  *tablespoons butter*
  ¼  *cup dry red wine*
  ½  *cup strong coffee*
  12  *medium-size mushrooms, thinly sliced*
       *garlic salt, to taste*
       *pepper, to taste*

Sprinkle sliced liver with garlic salt and pepper, and set meat aside while you prepare sauce.

In small, heavy saucepan, sauté sliced onion in butter over low heat. Stir occasionally, until onion is translucent and golden yellow.

Add wine and coffee to sautéed onion. Bring to a boil.

Reduce heat and simmer, until liquid reduces to about ½ cup.

Slice fresh mushrooms very thin, and add to sauce.

Butter a skillet and heat slightly. Put in liver slices. Immediately add sauce, and cook over low heat for 10-15 minutes, turning liver several times.

Serve liver garnished with sauce.

Makes 2 servings.

*Note: Liver will be tender and slightly pink inside.*

## beef goulash

   4 *lbs. beef chuck, cut into cubes*
 ½ *cup flour*
   1 *tablespoon garlic salt*
 ½ *teaspoon black pepper*
   1 *stick butter*
   3 *tablespoons paprika, preferably Hungarian*
   4 *cups onions, sliced thin*
   2 *cloves garlic*
 ¾ *teaspoon meat paste*
   1 *cup water*
   1 *cup very strong coffee*
 ¼ *cup sour cream*

Dust beef lightly in flour, garlic salt, and pepper.

Brown meat evenly in butter, in large kettle. While meat is browning, sprinkle with paprika.

Add onion slices, garlic cloves, meat paste, coffee, and water. Cover and simmer gently for 2 hours, or until beef is fork-tender.

Just before serving, stir in sour cream.

Serve over hot noodles.

Makes 8 servings.

## venison stew

         3  lbs. venison, cubed
            flour, to dredge
         1  teaspoon salt
       ½  teaspoon pepper
         2  teaspoons garlic powder
       ¼  cup vegetable oil
         2  medium-sized onions, chopped
         6  carrots, sliced thin
         1  teaspoon basil
      1¼  cups very strong coffee
       ¾  cup beef consommé
       ½  lb. thinly-sliced mushrooms,
            (preferably fresh)

Cut venison into cubes, about 1-1½ inches. Trim off all fat.

Dredge meat in flour seasoned with salt, pepper, and garlic powder. Brown in vegetable oil.

Remove meat from oil, and measure out 1 tablespoon of pan drippings.

Replace meat and add onions, carrots, and basil.

Combine coffee and consommé and add to meat and vegetables. Cover and simmer for about 1 hour.

Add sliced, fresh mushrooms and continue to simmer for 30 minutes, or until meat is fork-tender. If necessary, season with additonal salt and pepper to taste. If juice is not thick enough, thicken with paste made from just a little flour, garlic, and water.

Serves 6.

## baked chicken fazenda

         2  broiling chickens, quartered
            salt and pepper, to taste
       ½  stick butter
       ½  cup strong coffee
       ½  cup honey
      1¼  teaspoons dry mustard
       ¼  cup vinegar
       ½  cup brown sugar
         1  can Mandarin oranges

In shallow baking pan, arrange chicken pieces, leaving enough space around each to insure even browning. Season with salt and pepper. Bake at 350° for 35 minutes.

While chicken is baking, prepare the glaze. Combine butter, coffee, honey, mustard, and vinegar in a small saucepan. Stir over low heat until butter melts.

Add brown sugar, and continue to stir until sugar is completely dissolved.

Remove glaze from heat and cool to room temperature.

When chicken has baked for 35 minutes, brush on glaze liberally, and continue baking and basting until chicken is brown and crispy on the outside, about 15-20 minutes.

Remove chicken from oven and arrange on serving platter. Garnish with mandarin orange slices, if desired.

Serves 8.

## coffee-peanut rib, or chicken barbecue sauce

4 tablespoons peanut oil
¼ cup finely-chopped onions
2 cloves garlic, minced
¼ cup peanut butter
1 8-oz. can tomato sauce
1 tablespoon sugar
1 tablespoon vinegar
1 teaspoon, or more, chili powder, to taste
1 cup very strong coffee

Heat oil in pan. Add onion and garlic. Cook until translucent, BUT NOT BROWNED.

Add remaining ingredients, and stir to blend. Simmer covered for 5 minutes longer.

Use as a basting sauce and/or marinade for spare-ribs or chicken.

Makes about 2 cups of sauce.

## veal and ham casserole

3 lbs. stewing veal, cubed
½ lb. raw smoked ham, diced
¼ cup flour
2 tablespoons butter
½ cup onion, chopped fine
1 cup strong coffee
1 teaspoon ground cloves
1 cup hot water
½ cup dry white wine
2 cups potatoes, diced
2 teaspoons salt
¼ teaspoon pepper
1½ teaspoons Worcestershire sauce
¼ cup celery, sliced thin
  baking powder biscuit mix
  (optional for topping)

Cut veal into 1-inch cubes, and dice ham.

Roll the meat in flour and brown evenly in butter.

Remove the browned meat from the pan and sauté the chopped onion, until it is golden, BUT NOT BROWNED.

Drain the butter from pan and add the cloves, coffee, water, and wine. Simmer liquid for about 5 minutes, stirring to loosen browned meat particles from sides of pan.

Place meat in a 3-quart casserole, mixing the ham and veal thoroughly. Pour liquid over meat and add potatoes, salt and pepper, celery, and Worcestershire sauce. Cover and bake at 325° for about 1¼ hours, or until meat is fork-tender.

Remove meat from oven and top with biscuits, if desired.

Return to oven, uncovered, to bake at 450°, for 12 minutes, or until biscuits are golden brown.

Serves 6 generously.

## ham glaze with coffee

¼ cup strong coffee
¼ cup dry sherry
½ cup maple syrup*
½ cup brown sugar
1 tablespoon lemon juice
½ cup macerated raisins (optional)

Soak raisins in 1 cup of water or sherry for 1 hour before making glaze. Drain.

Combine all ingredients in heavy saucepan. Stir over low heat until thoroughly blended. Makes about 1 cup.

*Liquid brown sugar or molasses may be substituted.

## barbecued short ribs

3 lbs. short ribs, cut into 3-inch pieces
2 tablespoons vegetable oil
2 medium onions, minced
3 tablespoons brown sugar
3 tablespoons vinegar
½ cup strong coffee
1 cup catsup
1¼ teaspoons dry mustard
2 teaspoons salt
¼ teaspoon pepper
1 tablespoon flour

In large, heavy skillet, brown ribs in vegetable oil.

Add onions and brown, DO NOT BURN, in pan with meat.

Add the brown sugar, vinegar, coffee, catsup, mustard, salt, and pepper.

Cover and simmer over low heat until tender, about 1½ hours. Remove from pan and keep warm.

Skim fat from pan and thicken remaining juices with tablespoon of flour blended with a little cold water.

Spoon gravy over meat. Delicious served over rice.

Serves 4.

## hacienda hasenpfefer

5-6 *lbs. rabbit, cut into serving portions*
  2 *cups vinegar*
  2 *cups strong coffee*
  1 *tablespoon salt*
  1 *teaspoon peppercorns*
  1 *large onion, thin-sliced*
  8 *whole cloves*
  1 *bay leaf*
½ *teaspoon tarragon*
½ *teaspoon basil*
  2 *carrots, shredded*
  2 *cups water*
  2 *cups strong coffee*

    *Sauce:*
  1 *cup finely-chopped onions*
  2 *tablespoons butter*
  2 *tablespoons flour*
  2 *tablespoons granulated brown sugar*
⅔ *cup sour cream*

In large bowl, or crock, place pieces of rabbit. Cover with coffee, vinegar, salt, peppercorns, onion, cloves, bay leaf, tarragon, basil, and carrots. Cover and marinate for 24 hours, turning meat occasionally.

Remove rabbit meat, and shake off excess marinade.

Place meat in kettle and add water-and-coffee mixture. Cover, bring to boil, reduce heat, and simmer for 2 hours.

Remove rabbit and keep warm. Reserve 2 cups of broth, measured.

*Sauce:*
Sauté finely-chopped onion in butter until translucent. DO NOT BROWN.

Make a paste of flour with a few teaspoons of broth and brown sugar. Blend paste into 2 cups of broth and cook until thickened. Adjust seasonings to taste.

Reduce heat. Blend in sour cream, being careful not to overheat, or sour cream will curdle.

Pour sauce over rabbit. If desired, sprinkle with chopped parsley. Serve immediately.

Serves 4-6.

## ham loaf with coffee glaze

      1  lb. lean smoked ham, ground
      1  lb. lean fresh pork, ground
    ¾  cup flavored bread crumbs
    ¼  cup onion, chopped fine
      2  eggs, well beaten
    ¾  teaspoon garlic salt
    ½  cup milk
    ½  cup strong coffee
      2  tablespoons parsley flakes

        Glaze:
    ½  cup brown sugar, firmly packed
    ½  cup honey
    ¼  cup strong coffee
    ⅛  cup vinegar
      2  teaspoons dry mustard

*This is a particularly delicious main dish!*

Mix ground meats together with bread crumbs.
Add onion, well-beaten eggs, garlic salt, milk,
coffee, and parsley. Mix until thoroughly blended.

Shape into a loaf and place in a 9 x 5 x 2¾-inch
loaf pan. Bake at 350° for about 30 minutes.

Meanwhile, make glaze.

*Glaze:*

Combine all five ingredients in a saucepan. Bring
to a boil over medium heat and continue to boil
for 1 minute.

Remove loaf from oven and baste with coffee
glaze.

Return to oven and continue baking for 1 hour.
Baste with remaining glaze after the loaf has
baked 30 minutes longer.

Turn loaf out of pan while still warm. Serve hot
or cold.

Serves 8.

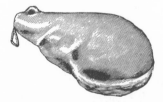

## near eastern fish broil

1 *lb. flounder fillets*
2 *tablespoons soy sauce*
4 *tablespoons black coffee*
½ *teaspoon ginger*
½ *teaspoon ground cloves*
2 *tablespoons light brown sugar*
3 *tablespoons salad oil*
2 *medium onions, sliced thin*

Mix together soy sauce, coffee, ginger, cloves, brown sugar, and salad oil.

Wash the fish fillets and place them in shallow baking dish. Pour sauce over fish. Cover with sliced onions.

Cover the baking dish with aluminum foil and refrigerate for at least 2 hours, turning occasionally.

When ready to cook, lift fish out of dish with slotted spoon, and place fillets on a sheet of aluminum foil on broiler rack. Spoon some of marinade over fish.

Broil quickly until golden. DO NOT TURN.

Serves 4.

## veal chops
## with onion sauce caribe

4 *large veal chops*
4 *tablespoons butter*
1 *teaspoon salt*
⅛ *teaspoon pepper*
6 *medium onions, sliced*
3 *tablespoons flour*
¼ *cup tomato sauce*
1 *small bay leaf, crumbled fine*
¼ *teaspoon marjoram*
¼ *teaspoon thyme*
4 *beef bouillon cubes*
1 *cup water*
2 *cups coffee*

Brown chops in butter. Remove chops from skillet and place in a 2-quart casserole. Sprinkle evenly with salt and pepper. Set aside.

Sauté onions in the skillet until golden brown, BUT NOT BURNED.

Blend in flour and tomato sauce. Add marjoram, thyme, bay leaf, bouillon cubes, water, and coffee. Stir constantly until mixture comes to boil.

Pour sauce over chops, cover, and bake at 350° for about 35 minutes, or until chops are tender.

Serves 4.

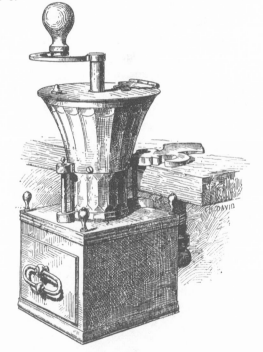

## sea island ham casserole

2 *cups cooked ham, cubed*
1 *cup cooked chicken, diced*
3 *large yams, parboiled*
1 *tablespoon cornstarch*
¼ *cup brown sugar, firmly packed*
¼ *teaspoon ground cloves*
¼ *teaspoon cinnamon*
1½ *teaspoons grated orange peel*
⅔ *cup orange juice*
1 *cup coffee*

Parboil yams until almost done. Peel, and slice lengthwise into quarters. While yams are boiling, make sauce.

Make paste of cornstarch and 3 tablespoons orange juice. Mix until smooth.

In small saucepan, combine cornstarch, remaining juice, coffee, orange rind, brown sugar, cloves, and cinnamon.

Cook over low heat, stirring constantly, until sauce is thick and clear. Remove from heat.

In a 2-quart casserole, arrange yams, ham, and chicken, alternating the ingredients evenly. Pour sauce over the mixture, making sure that all the ingredients are covered with the sauce.

Bake casserole at 350° for 20-30 minutes.

Delicious served on a bed of rice.

Serves 4.

# bake with coffee
## Breads, Cakes and Pastries, Cookies and Bars

*Nothin' says lovin'*
*like something from the oven.*
        —Pillsbury slogan

# breads

## coffee griddle cakes

1¼ cups all-purpose flour
1½ teaspoons baking powder
¼ teaspoon salt
2 teaspoons instant coffee
1 teaspoon nutmeg
½ teaspoon cinnamon
1 egg, well-beaten
1¼ cups milk
2 tablespoons melted butter

In large bowl, mix dry ingredients together.

In a separate bowl, beat the egg well. Add milk and butter to the egg. Stir to blend.

Make a well in the dry ingredients and pour in liquids, stirring lightly until blended. DO NOT BEAT BATTER.

Bake on a well-greased hot griddle until golden.

Serves 2 generously.

## spiced coffee loaf

2¼ cups sifted all-purpose flour
1 teaspoon baking powder
¾ teaspoon baking soda
1 teaspoon salt
½ teaspoon ground cinnamon
½ teaspoon ground cloves
¼ teaspoon ground ginger
1 cup sugar
⅓ cup (⅔ stick) butter
2 eggs
⅓ cup honey
1½ teaspoons grated orange rind
½ cup strong, cold coffee
½ cup chopped walnuts

Sift flour, and measure out 2¼ cups. Resift flour combined with baking powder, baking soda, salt, and spices.

In large bowl, cream together butter and sugar. Mix in unbeaten eggs, stirring until well blended.

Add honey and orange rind; beat vigorously.

Add coffee alternately with dry ingredients. Beat until batter is smooth and creamy.

Add walnuts and pour into well-greased 9 x 5 x 3-inch loaf pan.

Bake at 325°, for 1 hour and 20 minutes, or until wooden toothpick inserted in center comes out clean.

Loosen loaf around edges with a sharp knife, and turn out, right side up, onto wire rack to cool.

Wrap loaf in waxed paper or foil. Store overnight to mellow spice flavors.

Cut into thin slices to serve.

## easy-does-it raisin bread

1 *13¾ oz. package hot roll mix*
1 *cup strong coffee, lukewarm*
1 *egg*
⅓ *cup peanut butter*
½ *cup raisins*

Dissolve yeast from mix package in lukewarm coffee. Stir in egg.

Cut peanut butter into dry ingredients until coarse and sandy.

Stir dry ingredients and raisins into liquid. Stir until dough cleans bowl.

Knead dough on a lightly floured pastry cloth until smooth and elastic.

Cover dough, and let rise in a warm place until dough doubles in bulk.

Punch down dough on floured cloth and knead again.

Roll dough out into an oblong about 9 x 10-inches. Starting at the 9-inch side, roll up as you would a jelly roll, and place in a well-greased 9 x 5 x 3-inch loaf pan.

Let dough rise in warm place until dough again doubles in bulk.

Bake at 400° for 30-35 minutes, or until loaf sounds hollow when tapped.

Cool before slicing.

## Tilda's finnish coffee bread

  2 *cups (1 pint) milk*
  3 *eggs*
  ¾ *cup sugar*
  ½ *cup (1 stick) butter*
  1 *teaspoon salt*
  1 *teaspoon crushed cardamon (30 seeds)*
  2 *yeast cakes*
  ¼ *cup warm, strong coffee, sweetened*
6-7 *cups unbleached flour*
  ¼ *cup sweetened black coffee (glaze)*

Beat eggs slightly with sugar, crushed cardamon, and salt.

Dissolve yeast in ¼ cup of lukewarm coffee.

Warm milk over low heat, and stir in butter to melt.

Combine milk with dissolved yeast, and stir into egg mixture. Gradually add flour, kneading until dough does not stick to hands and is shiny and glossy.

Cover bowl, and put in a warm place, NOT HOT, until dough doubles in bulk.

Turn dough out onto floured board, punch down, and let rest for 15 minutes.

Wet hands and roll dough into ropes. Braid ropes and put on well-greased cookie sheet.

Bake at 375° for 20 minutes.

Remove loaf from oven and brush with ¼ cup sweetened black coffee, sprinkle with sugar, and return to oven for about 2 minutes, or until richly glazed.

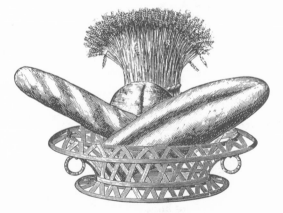

## date nut coffee loaf

1  1-lb. package pitted dates, chopped
2  teaspoons baking soda
2  cups strong coffee, boiling
½  cup (1 stick) butter
2  cups sugar
2  eggs, well-beaten
4  cups cake flour
½  teaspoon salt
½  teaspoon nutmeg
½  teaspoon cinnamon
1  cup chopped nuts
    (walnuts, pecans, or Brazil nuts)

Cut dates into fine pieces with scissors.

Dissolve baking soda in coffee, pour over dates, and let stand for about 15 minutes, or until coffee is cool.

Cream butter and sugar; add well-beaten eggs.

Sift together flour, salt, nutmeg, and cinnamon.

Mix about ¼ cup dry ingredients with chopped nuts. Set aside.

Add remaining dry ingredients and coffee alternately to creamed mixture. Beat until smooth.

Add dates and floured nuts. Mix thoroughly.

Pour into 2 well-greased loaf pans, 9 x 5 x 2¼-inches.

Bake at 350° about 1¼ hours, or until a wooden pick, or knife, inserted in center comes out clean.

Wrap in aluminum foil, and store in a cool place until ready to serve. Slice thin.

Makes 2 loaves.

*Note: Ideal for sandwiches, especially cream cheese.*

## hot coffee gingerbread

> ½ cup (1 stick) butter
> ½ cup sugar
> 1 egg, well-beaten
> 1 cup molasses
> 2½ cups flour
> 1½ teaspoons baking soda
> ½ teaspoon salt
> 1 teaspoon ground ginger
> 1 teaspoon cinnamon
> ½ teaspoon ground cloves
> 1 cup hot, strong coffee

*A delicious variation of an old favorite.*

Cream together butter and sugar until light and fluffy.

Add well-beaten egg, mixing well.

Add molasses and stir until well-blended.

Sift flour, baking soda, salt, and spices. Add dry ingredients gradually to creamed mixture, stirring until smooth.

When mixture is smooth, add the coffee and beat again until thoroughly blended.

Pour into a well-greased, lightly-floured 9 x 9 x 2-inch baking pan.

Bake at 350° for 30 minutes.

Cut into squares and serve hot. Also good cold.

Especially good with coffee whipped cream or coffee custard sauce.

## quick coffee rolls

> 2 cups sifted all-purpose flour
> 2 teaspoons baking powder
> 2 tablespoons sugar
> ⅛ teaspoon salt
> ¼ teaspoon cinnamon
> ¼ teaspoon nutmeg
> ¼ cup (½ stick) butter, melted
> ½ cup milk
> ¼ cup very strong, cold coffee
> 3 tablespoons sugar
> 2 tablespoons ground cinnamon
> ¼ cup (½ stick) well-softened butter

Sift flour, baking powder, sugar, cinnamon, nutmeg, and salt. Gradually stir in melted butter; mix well.

Combine milk and coffee. Stir into flour and butter mixture. Continue to stir until dough becomes smooth and stiff.

On floured pastry cloth, roll dough out into rectangle. Spread rolled-out dough with additional butter, and sprinkle generously with sugar-cinnamon mixture.

Roll as you would a jelly roll and cut in 12 equal pieces.

Place each piece in a well-greased muffin cup.

Bake at 375° for 10 minutes or until golden brown.

Serve hot with butter.

## coffee bran muffins

  1 *tablespoon melted butter*
¼ *cup superfine sugar*
  1 *egg, beaten*
  1 *cup whole bran*
½ *cup strong, cold coffee*
¾ *cup all-purpose flour, sifted*
½ *teaspoon cinnamon*
¼ *teaspoon salt*
  2 *teaspoons baking powder*
  1 *tablespoon raisins, chopped fine*

In large bowl, sift together flour, bran, baking powder, salt, and cinnamon.

Beat egg until frothy and lemon-colored. Add coffee, melted butter, and sugar, stirring to blend well.

Gradually stir liquid mixture into dry ingredients. DO NOT OVERBEAT. Add chopped raisins.

Line muffin pan with paper liners and distribute batter evenly in 12 muffin cups. Bake at 400° for 15 minutes. Serve warm with butter or cream cheese.

Makes 8 two-inch muffins.

## miniature coffee doughnut balls

    3 *eggs*
  ½ *cup sugar*
  ½ *cup corn syrup*
4½ *cups all-purpose flour*
  1 *tablespoon instant coffee*
  5 *tablespoons baking powder*
  ½ *teaspoon cinnamon*
  1 *teaspoon nutmeg*
  3 *tablespoons melted butter*
  ½ *cup milk*

Beat egg whites until stiff. Set aside.

In a separate bowl, beat the egg yolks until thick and lemon-colored. Gradually stir in sugar. Add corn syrup next and stir well.

Sift together flour, coffee, baking powder, and spices. Combine butter and milk. Stir the liquid into egg mixture, then add 4 cups of sifted dry ingredients. Mix well to blend, but DO NOT BEAT. Fold in the egg whites and add the remaining ½ cup of flour.

On a floured board or pastry cloth, pat out small quantities of dough to ½-inch thickness. Cut with a small round cookie cutter about 1½-inches in diameter.

Fry doughnut balls in deep hot fat, approximately 370°, until golden brown. Drain on paper towels.

Makes about 4 dozen.

## coffee loaf

  zwieback crumbs, rolled fine
2 teaspoons cinnamon
1 teaspoon nutmeg
2 eggs
2/3 cup sugar
3/4 cup corn syrup
2 teaspoons ground cloves
1/2 cup raisins
1/4 cup pecans, chopped fine
3/4 cup strong, cold coffee
3/4 cup (1 1/2 sticks) melted butter
1 1/2 teaspoons baking soda
1 teaspoon baking powder
2 1/2 cups all-purpose flour

Grease a 2-quart loaf pan liberally with butter. Sprinkle with a heavy layer of zwieback crumbs mixed with cinnamon and nutmeg.

Soak raisins in water until soft and plump.

Beat eggs and sugar together until frothy and lemon-colored. Stir in corn syrup, beating until well blended.

Add spices, raisins, and nuts, mixing well. Mix in melted butter and coffee; stir.

Sift flour, baking soda, and baking powder into mixture, stirring until blended.

Pour batter into loaf pan and bake at 350° for about 1 hour, or until knife inserted in center of cake comes out clean.

Let cake cool in pan. When cool, loosen at edges with a sharp knife. Turn cake out on foil.

Wrap cake in foil and age for 1 or 2 days.

Serve sliced with butter or cream cheese.

# cakes and pastry

## coffee cake

¼ cup (½ stick) butter
½ cup sugar
1 egg
1½ cups all-purpose flour
2 teaspoons baking powder
¼ teaspoon salt
½ teaspoon nutmeg
1 teaspoon cinnamon
⅓ cup strong coffee
⅓ cup table cream
1 teaspoon vanilla extract
½ cup mixed candied fruit, optional

Topping mix:
3 tablespoons light brown sugar
1 teaspoon cinnamon

In large bowl, cream together butter and sugar. Add egg and mix until well blended.

Combine flour, baking powder, salt, nutmeg, and cinnamon. Gradually add dry ingredients to creamed mixture, alternating with coffee, cream, and vanilla. Stir well, until batter is smooth and creamy.

If desired, add candied fruit lightly dusted with flour.

Pour into well-greased 9 x 5-inch loaf pan. Sprinkle with topping mix.

Bake at 375° for 40 minutes, or until golden brown.

Cool in pan, or slice and serve hot with butter.

## coffee cream roll

*Jelly roll batter:*
4 *eggs*
¾ *teaspoon baking powder*
¼ *teaspoon salt*
¾ *cup sugar*
1 *teaspoon vanilla*
¾ *cup all-purpose flour*

In mixing bowl, beat eggs with baking powder and salt. Set bowl over a pan of hot, NOT BOILING, water. Beat until foamy.

Gradually add sugar, beating until mixture is thick and lemon-colored.

Remove bowl from over hot water and add vanilla. Fold in flour.

Grease a 15½ x 10½ x 1-inch jelly roll pan. Line it with waxed paper. Grease the waxed paper. Pour batter into pan and spread evenly in pan.

Bake at 400° for about 12 minutes, or until cake springs back from the touch.

Turn cake out, upside-down, on a pastry cloth dusted with confectioners' sugar. Carefully remove waxed paper.

Trim the edges and roll up, leaving cloth inside.

Cool before filling.

*Coffee cream:*
1 *cup cream, whipped*
2 *tablespoons sugar*
2 *tablespoons very strong, cold coffee*

Whip cream. Add sugar and coffee, mixing to blend.

Unroll cake, and spread generously with coffee cream.

Re-roll cake. Slice and serve.

Makes 8 servings.

## coffee-peanut layer cake

¾ cup peanut butter
½ cup (1 stick) butter
1½ teaspoons vanilla extract
2¼ cups firmly-packed brown sugar
3 eggs
3 cups all-purpose flour
3 teaspoons baking powder
½ teaspoon salt
¾ cup milk
½ cup strong, cold coffee

Cream peanut butter, butter, and vanilla. Stir in sugar, mixing until well blended. Add eggs, one at a time, beating after each addition.

Mix flour, baking powder, and salt.

Combine milk and coffee.

Add liquid alternately with dry ingredients to peanut butter mix, beginning and ending with dry ingredients.

Pour batter into 3 greased and floured 9-inch cake pans.

Bake at 350° for 30-35 minutes, or until cake shrinks from sides of pan.

Remove and cool layers on wire racks.

Ice with coffee butter frosting.

## quick & easy raisin spice cake

1½ cups flour
1 cup sugar
½ teaspoon salt
1 teaspoon baking powder
1 teaspoon baking soda
¾ teaspoon allspice
½ teaspoon ground cloves
¾ teaspoon cinnamon
¼ teaspoon nutmeg
¼ teaspoon ginger
½ cup (1 stick) butter, melted
1 egg
1 cup strong coffee
½ cup seedless raisins

Sift flour, sugar, salt, baking powder, baking soda, and spices into a large mixing bowl. Add butter, unbeaten egg, and coffee. Beat vigorously, until batter is smooth.

Dust raisins in flour and mix into batter.

Pour into a greased 8 x 8 x 2-inch baking pan. Bake at 350° for 35-40 minutes, or until a toothpick inserted in the center comes out clean.

Cool on wire rack.

If desired, top with coffee frosting.

Makes 6 servings.

## coffee cream pancake

### (oven-baked)

  1  *teaspoon butter*
  2  *eggs*
¼  *cup sugar*
  3  *tablespoons very strong, cold coffee*
¾  *cup heavy cream, whipped*
½  *cup all-purpose flour, sifted*
¼  *teaspoon salt*

Grease a 9-inch baking pan with butter.

In large bowl, beat eggs, sugar, and coffee until thick and frothy. Fold in whipped cream. Stir in sifted flour and salt, beating rapidly until smooth.

Pour at once into baking pan, and bake at 350° for 30-40 minutes.

Cool in pan.

Cut into rectangular serving pieces.

Makes 6 servings.

*Note: Pancake is delicious topped with coffee whipped cream topping or your favorite jam.*

## mocha cake

½ cup very hot, strong coffee
2 oz. unsweetened chocolate, chopped fine
½ cup (1 stick) butter
2 cups brown sugar
2 eggs
2 cups all-purpose flour
1 teaspoon baking soda
½ teaspoon salt
½ cup buttermilk
1 teaspoon vanilla extract

*This cake is superb with coffee cream frosting. A sure-fire treat for everyone!*

Pour coffee over chopped chocolate, and stir until chocolate has melted.

Cream butter and brown sugar. Add eggs, one at a time, beating well after each addition.

Sift together flour, salt, and baking soda. Add dry ingredients to butter mixture, alternating with the buttermilk.

Add coffee mixture and vanilla extract. Mix well, until smooth.

Pour batter into a greased, waxed paper-lined 8 x 8 x 2-inch baking pan.

Bake at 325° for 30 minutes, or until middle of cake springs back to the touch.

Remove cake from oven and cool in pan for a few minutes.

Turn cake out on wire rack, upside down. Carefully remove waxed paper, and cool.

Ice with your favorite frosting.

Makes 6 servings.

## coffee cream puffs

*Pastry:*
½ *cup (1 stick) butter*
½ *cup cold, black coffee*
½ *cup water*
¼ *teaspoon salt*
½ *teaspoon nutmeg*
1 *teaspoon ground cloves*
1 *cup sifted flour*
4 *eggs*

Grease a large cookie sheet.

In medium saucepan, over medium heat, combine water, butter, and salt. Heat until water boils and butter melts. Remove from heat.

Add spices and sifted flour all at once, mixing well until mixture leaves sides of pan.

Add eggs one at a time, beating until smooth after each addition. Continue to beat dough until it is smooth and shiny.

Using a tablespoon, make little balls, and drop them on greased cookie sheet about 2 inches apart.

Bake at 450° for 15 minutes.

Reduce heat to 350° and continue baking for about 30 minutes, or until golden.

Remove puffs from oven, and cool on a wire rack. Cut thin layer from tops, and save.

Scoop out any unbaked dough. Fill with coffee whipped cream.

Makes about a dozen puffs.

*Coffee whipped cream:*
1 *cup heavy cream, whipped*
6 *tablespoons of very strong coffee*
  *sugar to taste*

Whip cream, and add coffee slowly to cream. Add sugar, stirring to blend well.

Spoon into cream puff shells and replace tops.

## penny-pincher's fruit cake

### (baking time: 2½ hours)

```
    1  lb. very fat salt pork, ground fine
    1  cup boiling water
    1  cup molasses
    1  tablespoon vanilla
 1½  cups hot, black coffee
    2  cups dark brown sugar
    7  cups all-purpose flour, sifted
    1  lb. seedless raisins
    1  lb. currants
  ¼  lb. mixed candied fruit
    1  cup finely-chopped mixed nuts
    1  tablespoon ground cloves
    2  teaspoons cinnamon
    1  teaspoon nutmeg
    1  teaspoon ground ginger
  ½  teaspoon salt
  ½  teaspoon baking soda
    2  tablespoons baking powder
```

In food processor or mill, grind salt pork very fine. Cover salt pork with boiling water and coffee. Set it aside to cool.

When mixture is cool, stir in molasses and sugar; mix well. Add vanilla and coffee.

Dredge currants, raisins, nuts, and candied fruit in 1 cup of flour. Set aside in a small bowl.

Sift remaining flour with cloves, cinnamon, nutmeg, ginger, salt, baking soda, and baking powder.

Check liquid mixture to make certain sugar is thoroughly dissolved, then gradually add dry ingredients, beating well until smooth and creamy in texture. Add fruits and nuts and stir well, to distribute evenly in batter.

Line a deep 10-inch tube pan with two thicknesses of brown kitchen paper. Grease thoroughly.

Begin baking in a very slow oven, 275°, for 30 minutes; increase oven heat to 300° for the next 30 minutes.

Increase heat again to 325°, and continue baking for 1½ hours. Place a pan of hot water in oven while cake is baking, to keep cake moist.

Loosen cake from edges with sharp knife. Turn cake out on a wire rack and cool completely.

Wrap cake carefully in aluminum foil and store in a cool place for several days before serving.

If desired, make brandy fruitcake, by wrapping cake in brandy-soaked cheesecloth before wrapping in aluminum foil.

Makes about 20 servings.

## coffee spice cupcakes

   1 tablespoon melted butter
   1/2 cup superfine sugar
   1 egg
   1/2 cup strong, cold coffee
   1 cup all-purpose flour, sifted
   2 teaspoons baking powder
   1/4 teaspoon nutmeg
   1/4 teaspoon ginger
   1/4 teaspoon allspice
   1/2 teaspoon cinnamon
   1/4 teaspoon salt
   1/2 teaspoon vanilla extract

In large bowl, sift all dry ingredients together.

Beat egg until frothy and lemon-colored. Add coffee, sugar, melted butter, and vanila extract.

Gradually stir egg and coffee mixture into dry ingredients, beating until smooth.

Line 8 muffin cups with paper lining cups and distribute cake batter equally among them.

Set muffin pan in a shallow pan of water. Cover muffin tin with aluminum foil or inverted rectangular baking pan to keep batter moist.

Bake at 350° for 20 minutes.

Remove cover, and continue to bake another 5 minutes, or until an inserted toothpick comes out clean.

Cool on wire rack.

Top with coffee frosting.

# cookies and bars

## coffee-glazed cookies

3 cups all-purpose flour, sifted
1 teaspoon baking powder
½ teaspoon baking soda
1 cup (2 sticks) butter
1 cup sugar
¼ cup cold, strong coffee

Sift together flour, baking powder, and baking soda.

Cream butter with sugar. Blend coffee into creamed mixture.

Gradually add dry ingredients. Mix well after each addition until dough is smooth.

Roll out dough on a floured pastry cloth, using about one-third portion at a time, to a thickness of ⅛-inch. Cut into crescent shapes.

Place crescents on ungreased cookie sheets and bake at 375° for 5-7 minutes, or until golden brown around edges.

Prepare coffee glaze.

Glaze:
½ cup sugar
⅓ cup strong coffee
¼ cup honey
½ cup finely-chopped walnuts

In small, heavy saucepan, mix coffee, sugar, and honey. Bring to a boil over medium heat; reduce heat and simmer for 5 minutes.

Brush glaze over warm cookies. Sprinkle immediately with chopped walnuts. Cool.

Makes about 5 dozen cookies.

## dropped coffee-ginger cookies

1¼ cups (2½ sticks) butter
⅓ cup brown sugar, firmly-packed
1½ cups molasses
1 egg, well beaten
5 cups all-purpose flour
2 teaspoons ginger
1½ teaspoons cinnamon
1½ teaspoons allspice
½ cup boiling coffee

4 teaspoons baking soda
½ teaspoon salt

Cream together butter and brown sugar. Add molasses and egg, beating the batter vigorously.

Sift together 2 cups all-purpose flour with the spices. Stir into the creamed mixture.

Add the boiling coffee and another cup of flour. Mix thoroughly and chill for 30 minutes in the refrigerator.

Sift the remaining 2 cups of flour 2 times with the salt and baking soda. Mix into batter, cover, and chill overnight. Letting batter stand will steep the spice flavors, and enhance the taste.

When ready to bake, soften batter to room temperature.

Drop tablespoons of batter onto a greased cookie sheet, several inches apart, to allow for spreading.

Bake at 350° for 8-10 minutes.

Cool completely. Store in a covered jar.

Makes 5 dozen.

## mocha-peanut chip cookies

¼ cup (½ stick) butter
¼ cup vegetable shortening
2 tablespoons peanut butter
½ cup granulated sugar
½ cup firmly-packed brown sugar
1 egg
1 teaspoon vanilla extract
1¾ cups all-purpose flour, sifted
½ teaspoon baking soda
3 tablespoons powdered instant coffee
½ teaspoon salt
1 cup chopped peanuts
1 cup semi-sweet chocolate chips

A scrumptious peanut butter variation of the favorite chocolate chip cookie.

Cream together butter, shortening, and peanut butter until soft and fluffy. Stir in sugars, egg, and vanilla extract.

Combine flour, baking soda, powdered instant coffee, and salt.

Sift dry ingredients into batter, mixing until

smooth and well blended. Fold in chopped peanuts and chocolate chips.

Drop teaspoons of cookie dough onto an ungreased cookie sheet, leaving about 2 inches between cookies.

Bake at 375° for 8-10 minutes, or until cookies are lightly browned around edges.

Cool cookies at least 5 minutes on cookie sheet before removing to wire rack.

Makes about 4 dozen cookies.

## coffee-peanut brownies

¾  cup peanut butter
⅓  cup (⅔ stick) butter
2  cups sugar
1  cup firmly-packed brown sugar
2  tablespoons powdered instant coffee
4  eggs
1½  teaspoons vanilla extract
3  cups all-purpose flour, sifted
1  tablespoon baking powder
1  teaspoon salt
¼  cup chopped, unsalted peanuts

Cream together peanut butter, butter, and sugars.

Combine eggs, powdered instant coffee, and vanilla, beating slightly to blend. Stir into creamed mixture, beating vigorously.

Sift dry ingredients and gradually add to coffee-peanut butter mixture. Beat until smooth. Stir in chopped peanuts.

Spread batter evenly into a well-greased cake pan, 9 x 13 x 2-inches.

Bake at 350° for 35 minutes.

Cool brownies in pan. Cut into rectangles to serve.

If desired, top with coffee glaze.

*Coffee glaze:*
2  cups confectioners' sugar
2-3  tablespoons very strong, cold coffee
½  teaspoon vanilla

Blend all ingredients until smooth and creamy.

Spread glaze on cooled brownies.

## oatmeal-coffee bars

    1   cup (2 sticks) butter
    1   cup brown sugar
  2½   cups quick-cooking rolled oats
  2½   cups all-purpose flour
    ¾   teaspoon salt
    1   teaspoon baking soda
    ½   cup strong, hot coffee
    ½   cup finely-chopped nuts

In large bowl, cream butter and sugar until light and fluffy. Add the rolled oats.

Sift flour and salt together.

Dissolve baking soda in hot coffee.

Add the sifted flour alternately to the butter-sugar mixture with the liquid. Mix well.

Chill dough until firm enough to roll.

Roll out dough on floured pastry cloth to a thickness of about half an inch. Cut into bars or squares.

Bake on a well-greased cookie sheet at 350° for 15-20 minutes.

If desired, glaze with coffee glaze.

Makes about 3 dozen bars.


    Coffee glaze:
    2   cups confectioners' sugar
    2   tablespoons very strong coffee
    ½   teaspoon vanilla

Blend all ingredients together until smooth and creamy. Add slightly more coffee if necessary.

Spread glaze on cooled bars.

## coffee cream horns

*The horns:*
5 *tablespoons superfine sugar*
2½ *tablespoons all-purpose flour*
2 *teaspoons instant coffee*
2 *eggs, unbeaten*
1 *egg yolk*

Using egg beater, beat together sugar, flour, coffee, eggs, and yolk, until mixture is thick and lemon-colored.

Grease a warm cookie sheet and drop 3 teaspoonfuls of the dough on it. DO NOT PUT MORE THAN 3 SPOONFULS ON COOKIE SHEET. Spread each spoonful to a diameter of 2 inches.

Bake at 400° for 4-5 minutes, or until golden at edges.

Remove cookies from sheet while still hot and roll immediately into horns.

Cool on ¼-inch wire rack and repeat process until all the cookies are baked and rolled into horns.

Cool and fill with coffee cream.

Makes about 4 dozen.

*Coffee cream:*
2 *cups heavy cream, whipped*
6 *tablespoons superfine sugar*
1 *tablespoon very strong coffee*

Whip cream until stiff and peaky. Stir in sugar until well blended. Add coffee and beat briefly to blend.

Spoon cream carefully into cooled horns and serve immediately.

## mocha squares

*Cake layer:*
1½ cups self-rising flour
1 cup shredded coconut
½ cup light brown sugar
¾ cup (1½ sticks) butter

Mix together all the dry ingredients.

Melt the butter and pour over dry ingredients.
Mix until well blended. Dough will be stiff.

Press dough into a well-greased baking pan,
8 x 8 x 2-inches.

Bake at 350° for about 20 minutes.

Turn cake out on wire rack. Cool.

When cold, top with mocha frosting. Let cake set
until frosting is firm. Cut into squares.

Makes 6 servings.

*Mocha frosting:*
4 tablespoons butter, melted
2 tablespoons strong, cold coffee
½ cup presweetened, powdered cocoa

Mix butter with coffee.

Pour over cocoa, and mix until well blended.

Spread frosting on cake.

# *perfect endings*

*Great is the art of beginning,*
*but greater the art is of ending.*
*—Elegiac Verse*
 Henry Wadsworth Longfellow

## brazilian banana fritters with coffee-rum sauce

Fritters:
1 cup enriched pastry flour, sifted
2 teaspoons baking powder
1 teaspoon salt
¼ cup superfine sugar
1 egg, well beaten
⅓ cup milk
2 teaspoons melted butter
3 firm bananas
coffee rum sauce (recipe below)

Sift flour, baking powder, salt, and sugar into a large bowl.

In small bowl, combine well-beaten egg, milk, and melted butter.

Gradually stir liquid mixture into dry ingredients, mixing until smooth and slightly stiff.

Cut each banana into four equal pieces. Roll in flour and coat evenly with batter.

Heat vegetable oil, using about 2 inches of oil, in a large, heavy skillet.

Drop fritters into heated oil, turning often to brown evenly.

Remove with slotted spoon and drain on wire rack.

Serve hot with coffee-rum sauce.

Coffee-rum sauce:
1 cup sugar
1½ cups strong coffee
2 tablespoons cornstarch
3 tablespoons cold coffee
2 tablespoons butter
2 tablespoons rum

Melt sugar slowly in pan, stirring frequently to prevent scorching. Gradually add 1½ cups coffee, stirring constantly.

Blend cornstarch with cold coffee to form a smooth paste. Stir cornstarch mixture into coffee mixture.

Continue to cook, stirring constantly, until sauce boils and thickens. Remove from heat.

Add butter and rum, stirring until butter dissolves.

Spoon sauce generously over banana fritters, and serve warm.

## mocha chiffon pie

1 9-inch ready-made graham cracker crust
2 envelopes unflavored gelatin
½ cup cold water
1 cup strong, hot coffee
½ oz. baking chocolate
⅓ cup sugar, plus ¼ cup additional sugar
1½ cups heavy cream
2 eggs, separated
1 teaspoon vanilla extract
⅛ teaspoon salt
1 cup heavy cream, whipped
    shaved bittersweet chocolate (garnish)

Soften unflavored gelatin in cold water. Add hot coffee, and stir until gelatin dissolves. Add chocolate, and stir until melted.

When chocolate has melted, add ⅓ cup sugar and ½ cup cream.

Pour mixture into well-beaten egg yolks. Cook in top of double boiler, over hot water, until mixture thickens.

Cool, add vanilla. When chiffon is almost set,

beat with rotary beater until light and fluffy.

Whip 1 cup of cream.

Beat egg whites with salt until stiff but not dry. Gradually add remaining sugar.

Fold whipped cream into coffee mixture. When thoroughly blended, fold in egg whites.

Pour into graham cracker crust and chill about 2 hours before serving.

Top generously with whipped cream. Garnish with shaved chocolate.

Makes 6 servings.

## coffee chiffon mold

  2 envelopes unflavored gelatin
1½ cups fresh milk
  ½ cup strong coffee
  1 cup light cream
  5 eggs, separated
1¼ cups sugar
  ½ teaspoon salt
    chopped nuts or
    grated bittersweet chocolate

Put gelatin, milk, coffee, and cream into top of double boiler. Heat over hot water until gelatin dissolves.

Beat egg yolks until thick. Add ¾ cup sugar to the egg yolks gradually, beating after every addition.

Slowly stir egg mixture into hot-coffee mixture and cook until mixture coats a metal spoon.

Remove mixture from heat and chill until syrupy.

Beat egg whites with salt until stiff but not dry. Gradually beat ¾ cup sugar into egg whites.

Fold egg whites into custard mixture and pour into a 2-quart mold.

Chill until set. Unmold on a large round platter.

Sprinkle with chopped nuts or grated chocolate. Decorate with whipped cream.

Makes 6 generous servings.

## coffee trifle

  ½ cup (1 stick) butter
  ½ cup granulated brown sugar
  3 egg yolks
  ½ cup strong coffee
    sponge cake, cut into squares,
    or 2 dozen ladyfingers
  ¼ lb. chopped Brazil nuts
  1 cup whipped cream
  4 tablespoons coffee liqueur

In large bowl, cream together brown sugar and butter. Add egg yolks, and beat until fluffy. Combine coffee with creamed mixture, stirring until well blended.

Arrange small pieces of sponge cake or split ladyfingers in the bottom of 1-quart serving bowl. Sprinkle generously with additional sweetened black coffee, to moisten. Spread cake with coffee-butter cream.

Continue alternating layers of moistened cake with butter-cream until all ingredients are used, ending with coffee-butter cream.

Top with coffee-flavored whipped cream. Chill at least 4 hours, or overnight. Sprinkle with finely-chopped Brazil nuts.

Serves 6 to 8.

## brandied bavarian cream

1½  envelopes unflavored gelatin
¼  cup lukewarm coffee
2  eggs, separated
¾  cup sugar
½  cup milk
2  tablespoons brandy
½  cup strong, black coffee
1  cup heavy cream, whipped
¼  cup finely-chopped almonds

additional whipped cream for topping

Soften gelatin in lukewarm coffee.

Beat yolks in top of double boiler. Add ½ cup sugar. Gradually add milk.

Cook over hot water, stirring constantly, until slightly thickened. Add gelatin mixture and stir until dissolved. Remove from heat.

Add coffee and brandy. Chill until mixture becomes syrupy.

Beat egg whites until stiff, adding remaining ¼ cup sugar by tablespoons, beating constantly.

Whip cream until it forms peaks. Fold whipped cream into gelatin mixture alternately with egg whites.

Pour mixture into a 1-quart mold that has been rinsed in ice water. Chill until firm, at least 1½ hours.

Unmold dessert. If desired, top with whipped cream or non-dairy whipped topping, and chopped almonds.

Serves 6.

## crêpes flambées
## with crème de brasil

*Crêpes:*
1 cup all-purpose flour
1 egg yolk
1 whole egg
1/2 teaspoon salt
1/3 cup milk
1/3 cup cold, black coffee
1 tablespoon lemon rind (optional)
1 tablespoon melted butter
1 tablespoon brandy

Combine first 4 ingredients, beating until creamy and smooth. Add milk and coffee gradually, stirring until well blended.

Pour the mixture through a very fine strainer. Add grated lemon rind, melted butter, and brandy.

Cook the crêpes, one at a time, in a well-buttered 6-inch pan over a fairly high heat. Tip pan around so that batter spreads evenly over bottom.

When lightly browned, turn crêpe and cook on other side. Keep crêpes warm.

Makes 12 crêpes.

*Crème de brasil:*
3 egg yolks
1/2 cup sugar
3/4 cup flour
1 teaspoon vanilla
4 cups milk
1/2 cup very strong coffee
1/4 cup brandy, warmed

Beat egg yolks and sugar, add flour, and mix well.

Combine milk, coffee, and vanilla in saucepan, and bring to a boil. Add egg, sugar, and flour mixture, stirring constantly, and bring to boiling point. DO NOT BOIL.

Spoon a small amount of thickened mixture into the center of each crêpe and roll.

Arrange crêpes in flameproof casserole dish, and sprinkle with sugar. Glaze under broiler.

Pour brandy over crêpes and ignite at table.

## mocha mousse

1 envelope unflavored gelatin
¼ cup cold, fresh milk
3 eggs, separated
3 tablespoons sugar
3 tablespoons powdered cocoa
½ cup coffee
1 cup heavy cream, whipped
   bittersweet chocolate

Soften gelatin in milk. In the top of a double boiler, over hot water, dissolve gelatin completely.

Beat egg yolks until thick and lemon-colored. Add coffee. Fold in stiffly-beaten egg whites, whipped cream, and gelatin mixture.

Spoon mousse into parfait glasses and chill for about 4 hours before serving.

If desired, top with whipped cream and sprinkle with shaved bittersweet chocolate.

Serves 8.

## dixie dandy cheese pie

1 3 oz. package cream cheese
1 cup confectioners' sugar
⅓ cup peanut butter
4 tablespoons powdered instant coffee
1 package whipped topping mix
½ cup milk
1 8-inch ready-made graham cracker crust
¼ cup finely-chopped peanuts

Whip cream cheese until soft and fluffy. Beat in instant coffee, sugar, and peanut butter, mixing until well blended.

Prepare whipped topping mix as directed on package.

Fold topping into peanut butter-coffee mixture, and pour into prepared graham cracker crust.

Refrigerate for 1 hour. Remove pie from refrigerator and sprinkle with chopped peanuts. Refrigerate again, until firm, about 1 hour.

Makes 6 servings.

## cold coffee soufflé

1½  cups strong coffee
1½  envelopes unflavored gelatin
  1  cup fresh milk
¾  cup superfine sugar
¼  teaspoon salt
  3  eggs, separated
  1  teaspoon vanilla extract
    whipped cream or non-dairy topping

Mix gelatin with coffee, milk, sugar, and salt. Place mixture in top of double boiler, and heat until mixture is scalded and gelatin is thoroughly dissolved.

Add 3 slightly beaten egg yolks. Cook over low heat until mixture thickens and coats a metal spoon.

Remove mixture from heat, add vanilla and chill until syrupy.

Meantime, beat egg whites until stiff.

When mixture is chilled, fold in egg whites.

Spoon into individual sherbet glasses and chill until firm.

Serve with a generous topping of whipped cream or non-dairy topping.

Makes 6 servings.

## plantation pie

(Prepare your favorite pastry recipe for a one-pie shell, or use a prepared shell.)

    Filling:
  1  cup heavy cream
  1  cup strong coffee
  6  tablespoons sugar
  3  tablespoons flour
½  tablespoon cornstarch
  5  egg yolks
⅛  cup dark Jamaican rum

In top of double boiler, combine cream, coffee, sugar, flour, and cornstarch. Bring mixture to a boil. Stir constantly, until mixture thickens.

Beat yolks until light. Yolks will be lemon-colored. Stir yolks slowly into mixture.

Cook over boiling water for 3 minutes. Add rum.

Remove from heat and cool to room temperature.

Pour filling into shell and chill thoroughly, at least 1 hour.

Top with whipped cream or non-dairy whipped topping. If desired, sprinkle with slivered almonds.

## *frozen mocha magic*

 1 3¾-oz. package chocolate pudding mix
 3 tablespoons powdered instant coffee
 ¼ cup sugar
 1 cup half-and-half
 1 cup milk
 2 cups heavy cream, whipped

Combine pudding mix, coffee powder, sugar, and half-and-half with milk. Cook as directed on package.

Cover surface with saran wrap and chill thoroughly.

Beat pudding until creamy. Blend in whipped cream and freeze for about 1 hour in a shallow, freezer-proof pan.

When frozen and firm, spoon mixture into a medium bowl. Beat until smooth but not melted. Mixture will be of frozen custard consistency.

Pour pudding and cream mixture into a 9 x 5-inch loaf pan.

Refreeze until firm.

If desired, top with hot fudge coffee sauce.

Makes 6 generous servings.

## coffee-rum ice cream

1  14½-oz. can evaporated milk, heated
5  tablespoons sugar
5  tablespoons strong coffee
5  tablespoons rum
2  cups heavy cream

Heat evaporated milk. Stir in coffee, rum, and sugar. Mix well to dissolve sugar.

Remove from heat and let stand for 10 minutes.

Add cream. Mix well to combine flavors. Pour liquid into ice-cube trays from which dividers have been removed.

Freeze until almost firm.

Unmold mixture into chilled bowl. Beat with a rotary beater until thick and fluffy.

Return mixture to trays and refreeze until almost firm. Beat again until smooth.

Put into freezable container and freeze until firm.

Makes about 1½ quarts.

## brandied coffee parfait

1  cup sugar
½  cup strong coffee
8  egg yolks
⅓  cup brandy
3  cups heavy cream, whipped
¼  cup brandy (for whipped cream)

Combine sugar with coffee in saucepan. Boil until syrup spins a fine thread.

Beat egg yolks until thick and lemon-colored.

Gradually pour hot syrup into egg yolks, beating constantly until mixture thickens. Continue beating until cool.

Add ⅓ cup brandy slowly, stirring to blend. Stir in heavy cream that has been whipped with remaining ¼ cup brandy.

Spoon parfait batter into freezer-proof parfait glasses or a melon mold. Freeze for about 3 hours.

If desired, top parfaits with plain whipped cream before serving. Sprinkle with shaved Brazil nuts.

*Venice was the birthplace of many elegant coffeehouses, such as the chic Café Florian.*

# *the tops*

*You're the top!*
   —Cole Porter, song title

## coffee custard sauce

½  cup sugar
½  cup corn syrup
⅓  cup strong, cold coffee
⅛  teaspoon salt
1  egg white
1  teaspoon vanilla extract

In small, heavy saucepan, combine sugar, corn syrup, coffee and salt.

Stir constantly over low heat until sugar is thoroughly dissolved. Continue to cook, without stirring, until mixture forms a soft ball when dropped into cold water.

Meanwhile, beat the egg white until slightly stiff.

Pour hot syrup mixture gradually over egg white. Beat constantly, until mixture becomes thickened and shiny. Add vanilla and cool.

Makes about 1½ cups sauce.

## coffee-rum sauce

*(delicious on ice cream)*

1  cup superfine sugar
1½  cups very strong coffee
2  tablespoons cornstarch
3  tablespoons cold coffee
2  tablespoons butter
1  tablespoon rum

Combine sugar and coffee in saucepan. Over low heat, stir freqently until sugar is completely dissolved.

In a measuring cup, blend cornstarch with 3 tablespoons cold coffee to form a paste.

Add cornstarch paste to coffee mixture in saucepan. Continue to stir until mixture boils and thickens. Remove from heat.

Add butter and rum, stirring until butter dissolves.

Makes 2 cups.

## coffee conserve normandy

**(serve as an accompaniment to ham or pork)**

- ½ cup apple cider
- ½ cup black coffee
- ¼ cup cider vinegar
- 6 whole cloves
- 1 teaspoon ginger
- ½ teaspoon allspice
- 3½ cups sugar
- 1 cup raisins
- ½ bottle fruit pectin
  cinnamon sticks

In saucepan, mix apple cider, coffee, and vinegar together with cloves, ginger, and allspice. Bring mixture to boil.

Remove pan from heat, cover, and let steep for about 15 minutes.

When spices have steeped sufficiently, add sugar and raisins to mixture. Stirring constantly, bring mixture to a rolling boil over high heat.

Add fruit pectin all at once, continuing to stir. Bring mixture to a boil again, and boil hard for one minute, stirring constantly.

Remove liquid from heat and skim off any foam with a metal spoon. Pour syrup quickly into sterilized jars.

Add a cinnamon stick to each jar and seal at once with ⅛-inch hot paraffin.

Makes 3 cups (24-oz.) of jelly.

## coffee syrup

**(tasty ice-cream topping)**

- ¾ cup strong coffee
- 2 cups light corn syrup
- ¼ teaspoon salt
- 2 teaspoons vanilla extract

In small, heavy saucepan, blend coffee, corn syrup, and salt. Simmer over low heat for about 5 minutes.

Remove from heat and skim. Stir in vanilla extract.

Cool to room temperature, then store in a covered jar in refrigerator.

Makes 2 cups.

## coffee-rum glaze

*(delectable topping for coffee meringues)*

  2 *cups confectioners' sugar*
  4 *tablespoons dark rum*
  ¼ *cup strong coffee*

Combine all ingredients. Stir until smooth and syrupy.

## coffee-marshmallow cream topping

  1 *cup very strong coffee*
  1½ *cups miniature marshmallows*
  1 *cup unsweetened whipped cream*

In small, heavy saucepan, combine coffee with marshmallows. Bring mixture to a boil over low heat.

Reduce heat to simmer. Stir constantly, until mixture is clear and creamy-textured.

Remove mixture from heat and chill in covered bowl.

Meanwhile, whip the cream until it is stiff and peaky.

Fold cream into marshmallow-coffee mixture.

Makes about 4 cups topping.

Serve with ice cream or as a topping for cakes.

## hot coffee fudge sauce

  2 *tablespoons very strong coffee*
  1 *cup sugar*
  ¼ *cup table cream*
  2 *tablespoons corn syrup*
  2 *tablespoons butter*
  1 *teaspoon vanilla extract*

In small, heavy saucepan, combine all ingredients, except vanilla. Cook over low heat; gradually bring to a boil, stirring constantly, until sugar is completely dissolved.

Continue cooking and stirring mixture for 4 minutes. Remove from heat.

Mix in vanilla extract.

Serve warm over ice cream or coffee cream puffs.

Makes about 1½ cups.

## coffee royal sauce

*(serve over vanilla ice cream)*

  ½  *cup sugar*
1½  *tablespoons cornstarch*
  ¼  *teaspoon salt*
  2  *cups coffee, piping hot*
  1  *tablespoon vanilla*
  ¼  *cup brandy*

## coffee cream frosting

  6  *eggs, well-beaten*
  ⅓  *cup strong coffee*
  ¾  *cup sugar*
  1  *cup (2 sticks) sweet butter*

Put eggs, coffee, and sugar in top of double boiler. Cook over low heat, stirring constantly until mixture thickens.

Cool completely.

Add butter to cooled mixture, and beat until thick enough to spread.

In small saucepan, combine sugar, cornstarch, and salt. Gradually stir in piping hot coffee.

Bring mixture to a boil over medium flame. Boil for about 5 minutes, or until mixture begins to thicken.

Remove sauce from heat. Stir in brandy and vanilla. Chill.

Makes scant 3 cups sauce.

# coffee confections

*All's well that ends well.*
    —William Shakespeare

## coffee caramels

    2  cups evaporated milk
    ½  cup very strong coffee
    2  cups sugar
    2  cups light corn syrup
    ¼  cup (½ stick) butter
    1  teaspoon vanilla

Add milk to coffee.

In small saucepan, boil sugar, syrup, and salt, until mixture forms a soft ball when a small amount is dropped into water.

Add the coffee mixture and butter gradually. MIXTURE MUST NOT STOP BOILING.

Cook, stirring constantly, to firm ball stage, about 240° on a candy thermometer. Add vanilla.

Pour candy into buttered square pan, about ½-¾-inch thick. Cool.

Mark candy into squares. Chill in refrigerator until firm.

Cut candy into squares. Wrap each square in saran wrap. Store in refrigerator until ready to serve.

## mocha fudge

    1  18-oz. package semi-sweet chocolate chips
    ½  cup condensed milk (do not use evaporated milk)
    ½  cup strong coffee
    1½ teaspoons vanilla
       dash of salt

In top of double boiler, melt semi-sweet chocolate. Remove from heat.

Add all other ingredients and stir until mixture is smooth and shiny.

Pour fudge into a wax-paper lined pan, 8 x 8 x 2-inches. Spread fudge evenly in pan.

Chill until firm, about 2 hours.

Cut fudge into squares, and remove from pan.

## coffee-peanut puffs

    2  14-oz. packages caramels
    ¼  cup very strong coffee
    1  10-oz. package miniature marshmallows
    4  cups chopped, unsalted peanuts

Melt caramels and coffee over low heat, stirring frequently until smooth.

Using a fork, dip marshmallows into caramel syrup, coating them completely.

Spread chopped peanuts on a sheet of waxed paper. Roll dipped marshmallows in nuts, coating evenly.

Place candy on fresh sheet of waxed paper and allow to dry at room temperature.

When firm, store candies in an airtight container until ready to serve.

Makes about 4 dozen candies.

## bôlas de café (brazilian coffee drops)

3 *cups sugar*
1 *cup strong coffee*
1 *cup milk*
2 *egg yolks*
3 *tablespoons honey*
1 *tablespoon butter*
1 *tablespoon all-purpose flour*
  *pinch of baking powder*

Mix all ingredients in heavy saucepan. Cook over low flame, stirring constantly with a wooden spoon until mixture forms a hard ball when dropped into cold water, or reads 250°-265° on candy thermometer.

Remove candy from heat and cool in saucepan by beating, so mixture does not become grainy.

Shape into twists and wrap each in waxed paper.

## mocha balls

1 *can condensed milk*
  *(do not use evaporated milk)*
1 *tablespoon cocoa*
⅓ *cup strong coffee*
1 *tablespoon butter*
¼ *cup shredded coconut*

Combine all ingredients in a small, heavy saucepan. Stir over medium heat until mixture thickens and pulls away from sides of pan.

Place candy mixture on a well-buttered plate and cool at room temperature.

When cool, form candy into small balls. Moisten hands so candy will not stick to them. After making each ball, roll it in shredded coconut, to coat.

Makes about 1 pound.

### no-cook coffee-peanut balls

  1 *cup chunky peanut butter*
½ *cup honey*
  2 *tablespoons powdered instant coffee*
  1 *cup seedless raisins*
1½ *cups shredded coconut*

Mix chunky peanut butter with honey and instant coffee. Stir well, to blend in coffee. Stir in raisins.

Spread shredded coconut on a sheet of waxed paper. Form coffee-peanut mixture into teaspoon-sized balls. Drop balls into coconut, and roll to coat completely.

Chill until firm, about 4 hours.

Keep refrigerated until ready to serve.

Makes about 3 dozen candies.

*Brazilian workers carefully hoe coffee on the drying ground.*

# *index*

Rabbit recipe
    hacienda hasenpfefer, 57

Sauce recipes, *see* individual meats;

Topping recipes

Veal recipes
Venison recipe

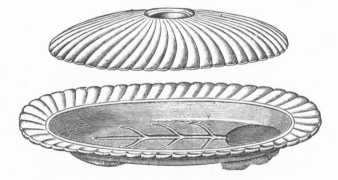